What Others Are Saying About
Little Athletes, Big Leaders

I just want to let you know, I can't put your book down and I continue to re-read many parts. My heart was actually racing as I read through some of your pages and I can't get enough of what you were writing and discussing. Thank you so much for putting together such a practical and valuable piece of reading and learning. Parenting is not easy and yet it is the most important thing I (we) will ever embark on and I love it. I so appreciate you taking the time to write this book and sharing your knowledge.

— BILYNDA WHYTING, M. ED

I LOVED your book! Nearly every page has something underlined, so for me that means it a good sports book! LOVED your pick of quotes!

— LINDA SHAFFELBURG

As a former high performance athlete, current high performance coach, and parent to two young children, I feel this book is an invaluable resource to parents who want to raise successful, happy, confident children, both in sport and also far beyond sport!

— CINDY TYE

I believe that all of us can benefit from the eloquently written points that you made regarding parenting and leadership! An excellent guide for raising successful children through sport — I highly recommend it!

— ROXANNE SEAMAN, PHD

This is one of the most influential books I have read, and is highlighted and post-it noted to pieces.

Jim Rohn, Randy Gage, Napoleon Hill are on my shelf and reading list, and Bruce, your book has joined them. I am grateful you followed your passion for growing little kids hearts, by letting us know what you know, through this book.

Thank you,

— DEBBIE FALCONER

I wanted to tell you that we were both very impressed and thought your book provided a lot of inspiration, even brought tears ☺ It reinforced some things I think we are both doing very well as a family as it also highlighted some things we need to work on as a family.

— VANESSA LANE

I think it's excellent. As a parent, I found it to be a bit of a wake-up call, and inspiring at the same time. It is very well-written.

— LEN PREEPER

Your book is excellent. Every chapter had an important message that I could certainly relate to in both my coaching career and my role as a parent. Every parent with kids in sport should be encouraged to read this book. I certainly intend to read it again, taking some written notes this time.

— BRIAN MACINNIS

I just finished reading your book, most of the time, either crying or with tears in my eyes, (thank you for that) It is TERRIFIC! My hope is that EVERYONE can experience reading it.

— CAROL WEATHERBEE

BRUCE BEATON
3-TIME CANADIAN FOOTBALL LEAGUE ALL-STAR

Little Athletes, Big Leaders

Effective Sport Parenting

Table of Contents

Raising Positive Children Through Organized Sport   ix

Introduction   1
    Is This Book for You?   2
    The Power of Repetition   3
    What is Your Goal as the Parent of a Child in Sport?   7
    Model the Way   14

Chapter One   19
    Unconditional Love   19
    Remove Their Greatest Fear   25

Chapter Two   33
    Focus on Transferrable Skills   33
    Find Transferrable Skills to Reinforce Daily   35
    Develop Your Child's Self-Discipline   41

Chapter Three   51
    Expectations   51
    Set High Expectations for Yourself and Your Child   52

Chapter Four   59
 Patience   59
 Choose the Slow, Steady, No Excuses Approach   62

Chapter Five   81
 Lead by Example   81
 Learn from the Experts   90
 Enjoy Moving Toward Your Goals Today and
  Every Day   92

Chapter Six   99
 Have Fun (and Eliminate Athletic Performance
  Anxiety)   99
 Enthusiasm is a Powerful Sports Leadership
  Attribute   101
 Effective Mental Programming for Young Athletes   105
 Enthusiasm Affects Who We Attract as Friends   107
 Become Your Child's Positive Inner Voice   110
 Put Yourself in Your Child's Reality   113

Chapter Seven   117
 Spend Time Together   117
 Sport Can Be Valuable Time Together   119
 Make Teaching Life Values Through Sport a
  Top Priority   121

Chapter Eight   125
 Allow Your Children to Influence You   125
 Communicate Daily and Share Experiences   127
 Learn From Each Other   128

Chapter Nine 133
Daily Improvement 133
Coaching and Parenting a High Self Esteem Child 134
Building Your Child's Confidence 138
Building Your Child's Mental Toughness
and Resolve 141

Chapter Ten 145
Cherish the Honor You've Been Granted 145
Set Clear Parenting Goals 146
Our Values 148

Appendix 1 153
Leadership Resources for Coaches, Parents,
and Mature Players 153
Principles of Team Leadership 155
Coach's Resource for Selection of Team Captains 157

Appendix 2 159
Chapter Notes 159

About the Author 165

Raising Positive Children Through Organized Sport

I have had the great luxury of playing a professional team sport into my late thirties. During that period I learned a tremendous amount about how to be successful, both in sport and life, from the myriad of talented coaches who influenced me, the hard working passionate players who impacted how I approached sport, and from the hundreds of successful athletes from other sports that I trained or networked with while playing competitively.

I am also a voracious reader; during those years I read exhaustively about how great players and great coaches went about the business of excellence. A large percentage of my learning over those decades stemmed from the diligent application of the timeless principles that made those winners so successful.

Now I'm immersed in small town community life with young children of my own, and I am witness to an amazing level of passion as parents strive to develop their children through team sport.

This book is an attempt to share the knowledge that I have gleaned through my experiences about how to be successful in sport with those passionate, caring parents who did not have the same degree of decades-long learning experiences in sport that I had.

These days I do more reading about parenting and leadership (leadership training is one of my day jobs) than I do about excellence in sport. Naturally, I wanted to balance my "sport" information with the best research available on raising positive, successful children in general, and so I have referenced many top experts.

This book is written:

for parents who want to raise successful, happy, responsible children — children with the skills to lead themselves and others forward to a brighter future,

and for parents who feel that organized sport can be an important contributor to that long-term goal.

This book is also for parents who want to raise children with the "winning mindset" sought after in sport at the professional level. The truth is these objectives can be reached simultaneously through effective parental reinforcement.

Organizations like the *Detroit Red Wings, Apple*, the *New York Giants, Royal Bank of Canada*, and topnotch universities like *Harvard* all want the same kind of people — hard workers with clear goals and dreams, people with high self-esteem and great interpersonal skills, young leaders with solid character and values.

Leadership, work ethic, interpersonal communication, and goal setting are all transferrable abilities and skills. They can be learned and developed in sport and easily transferred to any life application. My personal belief is that in our society today, the sport world is the best and most likely place a child will develop these critical life skills.

My objective in writing this guide is to combine the passion of the "sport parent" with the practical knowledge, tools, and skills I acquired over the years, and to help ensure parents that their passion is well used for the betterment of their child in the decade or so that their child will be involved in organized sport.

I want to pass along to the average parent some of the "approach oriented" secrets enlightened former professional athletes who spent years learning their craft teach their own kids.

My goal is to help concerned parents meet the parental goal of raising, through organized sport, positive, happy, confident, secure future leaders who might pursue their goals and dreams (whatever they may be) with passion. To this end result, *Little Athletes, Big Leaders* is structured with a variety of information and advice, and lessons learned, mixed with anecdotes and sections in italics that are directed specifically as a recap to parents who indeed want to be the best they can be through utilizing many of the techniques and strategies suggested.

I don't pretend to have all the answers. My two children are currently eight and six years old, and I'm in the midst of my "most important work thus far," but I firmly believe that through sports and the positive skills learned therein, children can and will be better prepared for life beyond the gym, field, or arena.

Best wishes to you and your family, and always remember that the secret to eventual success for you and your little people comes down to:

BIG DREAMS and small daily steps!

Sincerely,

Bruce Beaton
www.littleathletesbigleaders.ca
bruce@littleathletesbigleaders.ca

P.S. If you'd like to receive our inspiring and informative daily sport message about hard work, perseverance, courage and daily improvement join our blog at *www .littleathletesbigleaders.ca*

Dedication

I would like to dedicate this book to hard-working
volunteer coaches everywhere. You are community heroes,
and as parents of children in sport,
we owe you a very sincere THANK YOU!

Bruce Beaton

Introduction

"Tis the good reader that makes the book."
~ Ralph Waldo Emerson

I'm hoping you do more than read this short book. My real goal is to have you implement a strategy or two that will affect the way you raise your child through the experiential learning activity we call "organized sport". The chapters in this book contain simple action steps, all of which take only a moment or two, yet any one of which will have a profound impact on your child's development if done repeatedly as part of your daily parenting routine. All the action steps are free, but the results derived from implementation of them will be priceless. You really can raise your child so that you beam with pride and fulfillment every time you think back on the wonderful work you did as a parent.

IS THIS BOOK FOR YOU?

"Life is either a daring adventure or nothing at all."
~ Helen Keller

This book is written for parents who sincerely want to raise terrific kids, and who understand intuitively that organized sport can play a positive role in the achievement of that goal. It is for parents who take a "no limits" approach to raising their children, and thus want to raise children to become positive, motivated, happy, secure future leaders, both in their chosen sport and more importantly, in society in general. It is for parents who want to raise strong, confident children with high self-esteem and clear values and goals. It is for parents whose dream is to raise children who courageously pursue their passions and dreams and live life to the fullest.

"Character isn't something you were born with and can't change, like your fingerprints. It's something you weren't born with and must take responsibility for forming."
~ Jim Rohn

This book is based on the premise that the organized sport experience can propel the development of a child's character and leadership skills far more effectively when parents know what behaviours and results to support and reinforce, and what behaviours and results to ignore. It is for parents who are willing to support their child through

the organized sport experience by consistently supporting transferrable skill development to ensure their child
has the best opportunity possible to succeed in any future
endeavour.

THE POWER OF REPETITION

Repetition is immensely important as a teaching tool.
Many children play organized sport for over a decade, often
through the incredibly malleable, influential, important
years from kindergarten through high school.

Parents have thousands of opportunities to reinforce a
proven approach that will make their children successful
in any area of their lives . . . as long as they know what to
reinforce. The adjustments proposed in this book are subtle
and easy, but they will make an enormous difference in a
child's ability to achieve success in the future.

> *"Any idea, plan or purpose may be placed in the mind
> through repetition of thought."*
> ~ Napoleon Hill

Reciprocally parents also have an opportunity to reinforce things that contribute little, or in fact damage their
child's ability to transfer lessons learned from sport into
their efforts to become successful adults. Parents who inad-
vertently damage their child's ability to develop a "winning
mindset" in life by making inappropriate comments tend
to do so repeatedly, often thousands of times over the span
of a child's organized sport years, often without realizing

that they are doing so. Being aware of these potentially negative reinforcements is necessary to avoid discouraging children, or causing even more serious or damaging results and consequences such as self-effacement.

I had a former teammate who was a terrific athlete and a hard core, tough competitor. He was 225 pounds of quickness and strength, probably about five or six percent body fat, and he could play almost anything well. We used to play squash together in the offseason, and when he'd miss a shot or get caught out of position, he'd say all kinds of nasty things to himself. He would do the same thing when we played basketball, and when we lifted weights; he was always angry about his numbers. He was just so hard on himself it was sad. Sport was never fun for him. He battled and battled, but the stress was almost unbearable. He just didn't have a winning mindset. He never learned that sport (and life) are all about the approach you take; they are all about your effort and your attitude, and that when you are battling, the mindset of the champion directs you to find opportunities to succeed, not the opportunities to berate yourself.

He had never been taught to reset his emotions and to stay in the present. Unfortunately, *he had been taught early in life* that no matter what he did, it was not good enough unless he was getting *off the charts* outstanding results.

That is no way for an athlete to live — constantly putting him or herself in an emotional pressure cooker where he or she in fact fuels the fire. It is not a healthy, productive way to compete, and those negative, destructive mental habits are difficult to erase once they are programmed in.

I would not want my child, or any other child, to feel that way, for the long term effects can and will be felt long after the skates, cleats, or pads are put away. It is a tough way to compete and an even tougher way to live.

A better, more positive approach — the crux of modern sport psychology and the core belief of all high performance athletes is — you do your best every day; you really lay it on the line and challenge yourself to improve, and you live with the results. You learn to control what you can control, and let go of the rest; you can always control your mindset. You then transfer that approach to future challenges you will face in other areas of your life.

As a parent, your "coaching style" deserves to be examined carefully at least once, if not more than once. This book has been written to help parents do just that. Ninety percent of the character development work is already being done because organized sport teaches skills like goalsetting, interpersonal skill development, discipline, and the ability to have fun while working hard. Because there are already mentors such as coaches who volunteer to help teach and guide the child through the sport experience, parents need to know what they can do to accelerate their child's development exponentially with a minimum of focused reinforcement, and how they can complement all that is already being done to shape the child in the best way possible.

"The values learned on the playing field — how to set goals, endure, take criticism and risks, become team players, use our beliefs, stay healthy and deal with stress — prepares us for life."
~ Donna de Verona

All it takes for parents to exponentially increase the benefits of sport is a few positive "approach oriented" comments repeated daily. The life lessons learned through sport regarding character and leadership will become a *natural* part of a child's thinking pattern.

Your job as a parent is NOT to coach. That's the coach's job. Your job is to teach your child life skills by helping them interpret the short term results they get — both positive and negative — through their sport experience. You are their most influential teacher, and thus you get the most important job — teaching character through sport. Jim Thompson of Stanford University put it the following way:

"My two decades of working with sports parents has taught me that (coaching) suggestions from parents are often not well received by their child. Athletes get so much coaching already — from coaches, from teammates, from the game itself. When parents add to this flood of coaching, it often overwhelms the child, like the proverbial straw that breaks the camel's back."

Organized sport provides a terrific environment for growth. It is worth taking the time to think through the important principles and skills you want your child to receive from the experience. It is worth using the power of repetition to ensure your child hears the appropriate reinforcement from you, after every **character development session***, better known as practices or games.*

WHAT IS YOUR GOAL AS THE PARENT OF A CHILD IN SPORT?

Your goal should be to encourage and support an approach to sport that provides your child with a "success" blueprint that can be readily transferred to any future endeavor.

Leadership guru John Maxwell says, "Successful people make good decisions early in life, then manage those decisions for the rest of their lives". You and your child have chosen organized sport as part of your child's development. This book is written to help you manage that decision so that you maximize the potential return on that investment of time, money and focus.

Keep in mind that the potential impact of sport on your child's development can be huge.

Sport is a microcosm of the challenges presented in life. Consequently, when coached well, with the lessons reinforced and supported effectively by parents, the experience can literally teach children everything they need to be successful in any future venture.

Successful people take a successful **approach** to life. Their approach eventually gets them the results they want, and that approach can be learned by first becoming aware of actions, and whether or not those actions are leading to a more productive or less productive future.

I learned this lesson when I was just eighteen. When I first went to university I was so happy to be off the farm and away from the structure and discipline of our 18th century (it seemed to me) upbringing, that I didn't take a minute to think through how my daily plans could influence my long term education and career goals. I hung out with my friends in the lounge of the dorm. We stayed in and watched TV almost all night (I grew up with 2 channels, one fuzzy and one clear, so the twenty we had in 1986 blew my mind). I learned to play half a dozen new sports, and I even went to a few classes (mostly afternoon ones). Generally I did things that were fun or easy, and procrastinated on the things that were important or hard. Bad approach. Bad results. My marks reflected my approach, and I was no closer to my dream of getting off the farm than I was when I started.

Fast forward to summer; I am now a year older and still standing ankle deep in cow manure needing a better plan. I had felt that school was my only way out, but I wasn't exactly acing my courses, and I did not know which way to turn. I wanted to be successful, but at that point in time, I did not know what to do to succeed.

Incredibly I found a book in my house entitled, *How to Succeed in University*, and I read it. OK, I skimmed it. But guess what? I was introduced to my first ever "approach-oriented" success plan. The little book said you must decide on an approach and stick to it, and detach yourself from the results. The author was a C student in high school and a straight A guy in college, so as far as I was concerned he had a track record. He said that if he could do it, I could too . . . and **this is the important part — I believed him.**

The strategy that worked for him was to study one hour for every hour of class time, and to never, never, never miss a class. I repeat . . . never, never, never miss a class.

He also advised that a person should study what he or she is interested in. He suggested heading straight toward your passions, and following your intuition when it came time to select classes. He said never worry about whether you are smart enough or talented enough, rather set a goal to be the best student you can be within the time parameters set, so that you still have time for athletic and social pursuits. It was a cathartic moment — it was the first time I had ever learned to clearly decide, in advance, what price I was willing to pay to see what talents I had to offer, and to let those talents determine where they might take me. I detached from the results, and I felt the stress start melting away immediately.

I followed through like a champ. I was like the mailman when it came to hitting classes that year, and every year since. Through rain, sleet, snow, hail . . . didn't matter if it was an 8:30 a.m. class (gasp) I was there. I sat in a quiet part of the library with a stopwatch and clocked my hour (no daydreaming allowed; that was another rule). And sure enough, just like clockwork, the great marks, the scholarships, the awards, the accolades all started to show up. I consciously reaped what I was sowing for the first time in my young life, and an important lesson was being learned:

"Great results come from focusing on a consistent approach, not on the result itself."

The truth is successful people take the following simple approach in their lives:

1.   They accept 100% responsibility for their life.

2.   They set clear goals and make plans to achieve them.

3.   They work daily on their goals and plans.

4.   They detach emotionally from discouraging short-term results.

Successful parents know that they are responsible for helping their child develop into a responsible, mature adult capable of meaningful societal contribution. The astute ones often involve their children in sport as part of that development process. This book is designed to help parents by offering simple, proven strategies that will maximize the positive effect sport can have on the development of the child's character and leadership skills.

So as a parent, what is your goal? What
results are you trying to achieve?

When asked this question, most parents respond with non-material, self-actualization kinds of answers like, "I want my child to grow up happy", or "I want my child to feel positive and secure", or "I want to raise a kind child with great values."

According to authors Brian Tracy and Dr. Betty B Young, "the goal of parenting should be to raise a child with high self-esteem. Self-esteem is simply your reputation with yourself."

Dr. Wayne Dyer states that, "The goal of parenting is to teach children to be their own parent. Kids should learn to be as responsible as possible as soon as possible, and your job as a parent is to guide them in that process."

I believe that one of the goals of parenting is to raise happy children with high self-esteem who understand that they were born to make a positive difference in the world while doing something they love, and that their main job is to figure out what that is and how to do it.

What is your goal as a parent? Have you thought it through? Have you shared it with your spouse? More importantly, have you shared it with your child?

Once you identify what your goals are as a parent, it is important to think through how organized sport and its array of volunteer coaches can assist you in your efforts. As a parent, it's critical to think through what lessons and skills you want your child to develop from the experience of organized sport.

As a sports parent, take a moment to think through your goals. What results are you trying to achieve from the thousands of dollars and the countless hours of time required to support your child through the next ten or so years of organized sport?

In his wonderful book "Positive Sports Parenting" Jim Thompson states:

"The place where parent-athlete relationships usually start to go wrong is with goals. Parents often don't take the time to explicitly examine their own goals for their child in sports or ensure that their behavior is consistent with their identified goals . . . Nor do they consider that their goals may not match the child's goals."

So what are your goals for your child in organized sports? There are many to choose from:

- Become a better athlete

- Become physically fit

- Meet new friends

- Earn a college scholarship

- Become a professional athlete

- Have fun

- Win

- Develop social and interpersonal skills

- Develop a solid work ethic

- Develop unselfish teamwork skills

- Deal with temporary defeats without becoming "defeated"

- Learn to set goals

- Learn to achieve goals

- Learn to perform under pressure

- Become more confident

- Learn specific sport skills

- Develop healthy lifestyle habits

- Learn "persistent patience" (the secret to long term success in any endeavor)

As you review this short list, ask yourself the following questions:

On game day do I stay focused on my long-term goals as a parent and guide? Do I walk the walk, or am I just another crazy sport parent who frets over short term wins and losses, who yells at referees about supposed "missed calls", and who treats the youth sports /education experience like it's a win at all cost event?

Dr Edward Banfield studied "upward social mobility" for decades at Harvard University. He was interested in why some people were able to jump from poor to rich, from the trailer park crowd to the jet-setting, multiple houses around the world crowd. He cited one determining factor, which he called "long-time perspective", which he described as "one's ability to stay focused on one's long-term goals, even if these goals were years or even decades away."

Achieving your goals as a sport parent is no different than achieving upward social mobility. You have to think long-term, well beyond your child's results this weekend, this season, or even in the next few years. You have to think about what kind of adult you are raising, what kind of potential leader and societal contributor you are influencing with your sports related feedback.

John Wooden, renown for being one of the greatest coaches in history, won ten national championships in 13 years at UCLA. His amazing record of performance will probably never be equaled. Wooden was often asked, at the end of each season, to evaluate the job he did coaching that year. He would always reply, "I'll let you know in 20 or 25 years." As an educator and a coach in the high pressure NCAA sports world of short-term results, John Wooden was unparalleled in his commitment to maintaining a "long-time perspective".

MODEL THE WAY

It is good to remember that to be successful in life you have to take responsibility, then set clear goals. Parents as well as children need to know this as they are models for their children who often do as their parents do through imitation. Children generally model what they see, and react less effectively to what they hear, especially when the two contradict.

Why not set a goal to teach children by example, and then use your voice to question, guide, and connect?

This is important advice for all parents and coaches, as strong role models whose actions and words positively coincide make all the difference.

The best parents I've ever known personally (they now have five amazing grown children) are Tom and Sharon

Higgins. Tom was one of the eight head coaches I had in professional football, and he was the best of the bunch. He was a teacher by profession. He played college football under legendary Hall of Fame coach and "life mentor" Lou Holtz. He married a first-class educator, and both he and his lovely wife are lifetime learners. And isn't that again, what role models do? They are constantly open to new approaches, improvement, and learning life's lessons. They reflect, consider, and become aware of their actions and reactions.

One of the first profound lessons I learned from Tom came when visiting his house once when one of his children came over and asked a question. Instead of providing a readymade, cookie cutter answer he immediately asked in return, "What do you think?" And every time she provided an answer, he repeatedly asked a variation of that same question.

After she sorted out her own thoughts and left the room with her own decision, I commented, "You're not really in the advice-giving business are you?" Tom replied with a smile, "No, I'm in the parenting business, which to me is the *teach them to think for themselves, do for themselves, and trust themselves business.* If I give them authoritative advice, they will mimic that pattern later in life, replacing me with a new authority figure. I am interested in teaching them to lead themselves."

Even though I didn't have children at that point in time, I filed that conversation away for future reference thinking, "Wow, great coaching really does extend far beyond the playing field."

I also learned how important role modeling is in good parenting. Parents who are also life coaches strive themselves to become well in the following areas — mentally, physically, emotionally and spiritually. They learn to align thoughts, beliefs and actions with long-term goals. They discipline themselves to consistently take small daily steps that bring them closer to the finish line. They make each day count in their efforts to live the life they want, a life that reflects their highest aspirations.

As an adult and parent: *This is your primary work. Set clear goals in all areas of your life, and work toward them daily. Raise great kids by setting a great example.*

So, again, what is your goal as a parent? What results are you trying to achieve?

Your child's involvement in sport should fit seamlessly into your overall goal as a parent. Sport can become a huge ally in your efforts to raise a child with high self-esteem, who has great interpersonal skills, and who understands the goal-setting and goal-achieving process.

Sport is often called a microcosm of life. Thus, sport can be a highly beneficial dry run for the child's future life challenges when the sport process is clearly understood and supported effectively by loving, supportive parents.

This book is a tool for you, the caring, loving parent who wants to maximize your child's sports experiences with the goal of developing character and high self-esteem in a success oriented child who learns to set goals, function effectively in a team environment, overcome adversity and pressure, react appropriately to positive and negative feedback, and therein become a leader.

Most importantly, it is for the parent who wants his or her child *to **easily transfer those skills to future endeavors.***

Action Steps

Define what you are trying to accomplish as a parent. Complete *the following statement. I believe the goal of parenting is to:*

_____

_____

_____

_____

_____

_____

_____

_____

_____

_____

You will spend thousands of dollars and countless hours supporting your child through the organized sport experience in the years to come. An investment of that magnitude deserves some forethought. What are your top three to five goals or objectives? Decide right now what you are trying to accomplish so you can review this book in ten or twenty years and evaluate whether you were successful in your efforts.

Chapter One

We worry about what a child will become tomorrow,
yet we forget that he is someone today.

~ Stacia Tauscher

UNCONDITIONAL LOVE

It seems almost paradoxical for this to be the most important paradigm for parents who want to raise courageous leaders who are unafraid of challenges. After all, doesn't great character develop through adversity and strife? The short answer is yes, but not in the home, and not while children are young.

Children need to be nurtured first, challenged second. Praise is incredibly important in the early years, and life will do enough criticizing on its own without a parent having to worry about adding to it. It is a parent's responsibility to provide that secure place where strategies can be learned, and techniques developed so that a child can get a healthy awareness and acceptance of self.

Ross Campbell wrote about children having an "emotional tank" in his book *How to Really Love Your Child*. Basically a child (or an adult) has an emotional tank much like a gas tank in a car. Children run off the fuel in that emotional tank. And as you've surely noticed, playing a sport well requires a tremendous amount of energy, and thus a lot of emotional fuel. A child's emotional tank can be filled up with positive, enthusiastic, loving comments from parents or coaches, or it can be emptied with harsh words, negative comments or indifference.

This concept really resonates with me as a long time athlete. Other people, particularly parents, coaches, or teammates — could empty or fill your emotional tank, especially when you were young, with a negative or positive comment. Parents and coaches often have no idea how draining . . . how absolutely exhausting . . . negative comments can be, particularly when you've done your best, and you're tired, *and you were anticipating a positive response to your efforts*. It really does feel like someone sucked the life right out of you. As a father of young athletes I have viewed well-meaning parents criticize their little one immediately after practice in an attempt to teach and instruct, and I watched the crestfallen child's post practice energy drain away before my eyes.

I once had a position coach in my second year in the Canadian Football League who yelled negative, draining, confidence destroying garbage at us EVERY DAY. His favorite line was, "I could find five guys working at K-Mart who could walk out here and play better than you guys." Our emotional tanks were always on empty. We gamely trudged through the season, doing our best to be energetic, but it was very, very hard. We regressed as a group and a team through the season, and finished with the worst record in the league. Our position group was also the worst, statistically, in the entire league. It was the only year in my thirteen years in the pros that I did not improve, and aside from winning the cup a couple of times, the happiest day in my career was the day that tiresome coach got fired. I despise negative, emotionally draining coaching, whether it's from parents or coaches.

Most of the coaches I had, and certainly ALL of the best ones, adhered to the advice granted by the brilliant relationship expert Dr John Gottman from the University of Washington. Gottman and his team have been studying relationships for over thirty years, and their findings have been impactful in the areas of marriage counseling, leadership training, and professional coaching. Gottman and his team can predict marriage success or failure with over 90% accuracy based on what they call the "magic ratio".

The magic ratio is the ratio of positive comments to negative comments. When it is 5 to 1 or above, the relationship thrives. When it is below 5 to 1, the relationship begins to erode. He calls it the magic ratio because magic things really do begin to happen when relationships function at or above the 5 to 1 ratio, whether they are marital relationships, parent–child relationships, manager–employee relationships, or coach–player relationships.

Keep in mind that athletes who want to get better enjoy redirection. Practice session redirections and corrections are NOT considered negative comments. They are positive — they show that the coach is paying attention, that you "matter" as an athlete, and that you are an important part of the team's ultimate success. All athletes at the pro level know they're "on the way out" when coaches stop redirecting them in the myriad of little ways athletes crave.

The "magic ratio" is especially important early in the little athlete's experience. In Daniel Coyle's significant book *"The Talent Code"*, Coyle presents a study done in the early 1980's by Dr. Benjamin Bloom. Dr. Bloom led a University of Chicago team of researchers who analyzed the experiences of 120 world class swimmers, tennis champions, pianists, mathematicians, neurologists and sculptors. One of the factors Bloom's analysis covered was "initial education in their chosen field". Bloom's study concluded that, "The effect of this first phase of learning seemed to be to get the learner involved, captivated, hooked, and to get the learner to need and want more information and expertise." This study reinforces the point that teachers who are positive and fun can become the front end of the funnel that creates champions years later. These teachers and coaches make learning enjoyable, and create a lasting enthusiasm that helps children push through the inevitable struggles that occur on the long road to world class excellence.

Early in the sport experience, the emphasis has to be on igniting a lifelong love of sport, including a love of the practice and personal improvement process. Years later, as athletes mature and coaches enter the "refinement" stages of the athlete's development, coaches can be a little less encouraging and fun if they choose. The athlete is hooked — they love the game, and are becoming self-motivated. The coach can concentrate on information and correction more than encouragement and praise. For example, when the great John Wooden's coaching style was analyzed, less than 7 percent of his comments were positive, less than 7 percent were negative, and 75 percent were pure information, given in short bursts, designed to redirect the athlete's current action. This approach improved Wooden's teams daily, and as a former university athlete, I can tell you there is nothing better than someone who can direct you in such a way that you improve rapidly. You notice it, and you appreciate it. This useful information makes practice "fun" for the competitive maturing athlete.

Where does this leave you, the parent, as you watch your youngster in the early years of their sport experience? Perhaps you would be wise to concentrate, like the great early coaches in Bloom's study, on encouraging your child to get "hooked" on the sport. Focus on fun and positive encouragement for a few years. When you watch your child perform at practice or in games and you notice a flaw in their performance that you feel you MUST, in your COACHING BRILLIANCE, pass on to your loved one, please adhere to the magic ratio, and calmly cite all the positive things your child is doing first. Make it a fun experience first, a technical experience second, by adhering to the 5 to 1 ratio in the early years. Not only will you help foster a long term love of sport, this one bit of advice from Gottman's findings will transform your "sport parent" relationship skills so that you enjoy the long term, positive relationship you seek with your child. And in the short term, you will keep your child's emotional tank full to the max.

Gottman's magic ratio can even help you communicate with your parent's coaches or referees if you're one of those supposed "helpful" parents who can't stay focused on your own work, which is positively reinforcing your child and all the sport volunteers who are helping you with their development. Coaches and referees love appreciation as much as players. Thank them for their time, their effort, and their contribution to your child's development. We're all in the business of raising great kids, and everyone plays an important role in this long term goal.

Your children want to please you more than you can possibly imagine. World renowned psychologist Dr John Gray states, "Children are basically programmed with one prime directive. Deep inside they only want to please their parents." It is very important, as the most influential guide in your child's life, that you consistently reinforce positive behavior. Nothing will develop their self-esteem like the wonderful feeling that you are proud of them.

All great leaders have a quiet, still, secure place inside that says, "I am enough." Consequently, they do not become people pleasers. They learn to love themselves and respect themselves completely when taught that they really are enough, just as they are. Fortunately, this does not teach them complacency. This teaches them to function as a whole human being, as humans who are born with passions, desires, courage, and energy. All they need is a worthy goal, and they're off!

"Man is a goal seeking animal"
~ Aristotle

Unconditional love is the most important principle for all parents, everywhere. If you want to raise a leader who displays an elevated character, and you don't read any farther than this sentence, remember to:

- *love your child unconditionally*

- *spend time with him or her*

- *lead by example*

Unconditional love is often the easiest of these three principles to practice, once you understand how important it is, and how to regularly convey that message to your child.

REMOVE THEIR GREATEST FEAR

If you want your children to be successful in sport, they have to know you will love them the same amount regardless of whether they succeed in sport, or even play at all. If they love you (and most kids are capable of an encompassing love that belies their little bodies) the thought of letting you down (and losing some of your love) is paralyzing. They would rather quit the sport, and that's what they do when they believe the amount you love them is connected to sport performance. Often they don't have the power to really quit, or they don't want to confront that reality with you, so they quit TRYING instead. The fear of letting you down and losing your love becomes a paralyzing fear.

"Truly loving another means letting go of all expectations.
It means full acceptance, the celebration of another's personhood."
~ Karen Casey

The solution, like most of the answers in this little book, is simple but profound. When you put your children to bed at night, or at other quiet times during the day, make sure you tell them REPEATEDLY that you will always love them the same amount, no matter what. Put that love out there as an indisputable fact.

- *Tell them you don't care if they play sport or not — you will love them just as much either way.*

- *Tell them you love watching them play, and you love spending that time with them.*

- *Tell them you watch their every move out there.*

- *Tell them you're proud of them.*

- *Tell them they are getting better and better with every practice — and if they choose to keep working hard, who knows how good they'll become?*

- *Tell them they're here to do something special, something helpful to the world, and you feel so lucky and proud to be their parent.*

- *Tell them you don't know what they are here to give to the world, but it has something to do with things THEY love to do.*

- *Tell them you will love them forever, no matter what.*

Let them bask in the glow of that warm, secure place so that they can step out into the world, and into the sport environment, with COURAGE. The most important things in the world to them (your love and your approval) are not at risk when they play sport. They are free to test their limits and work hard, and have fun with an internal feeling of security that comes from knowing that "they are loved completely regardless of their results." This secure feeling will empower your child to take the necessary risks to be as great as he or she can possibly become.

Putting my children to bed and having a five or ten minute conversation with them just before they fall asleep is the best part of my day.

As an athlete I was taught about the power of the subconscious mind and the need to program that part of the brain for athletic success. The most effective time to do mental programming is just before sleep because the subconscious brain never shuts down. As an athlete this is when you want to visualize championships, visualize individual excellence, and visualize performing in a calm, relaxed, optimum performance state. As an athlete this is also when you want to "link" positive past performance with positive future performance. If you're not an expert on getting into the brain's "alpha" state (which is an advanced skill that allows you to effectively visualize) then the best way to mentally program naturally is to simply do it when you're almost asleep or barely awake.

As a loving parent, my children trust me. Prior to sleeping, they are very open to calm, quiet, loving conversation. They just want Mom or Dad to stick around as long as possible. So when I sincerely tell them I love them completely, just the way they are, they believe me.

When I sincerely tell them I feel like the luckiest Dad in the whole world because they are my children, they believe me.

When I sincerely tell them that God must really love me because why else would He give me such a special present, they believe me.

When I sincerely tell them they are here to do something really special in the world, and that it probably has something to do with helping people, and I wonder out loud what it is, they believe me, and they wonder a little too.

This is also a great time to remind your children of their successes and positive traits, either in sports or in general. I love talking to my little athletes, my little scholars, my little musicians at bedtime about some of the wonderful things they've done in the past during school, music lessons, or practices or games. They love feeling those positive thoughts, and being the star in their own stories.

Whatever you program into your child's mind just before bedtime bypasses the conscious mind and for hours affects the subconscious mind. You are your child's guide, the loving parent, the most important influence, and bedtime is one of the greatest teaching moments you'll ever have presented to you. Use it well!

A side benefit to loving unconditionally is that your child will mirror your love. A truism about love is that it is a gift you receive, and the only way to receive it is to give it. If your child is still a baby, you have an amazing opportunity to set the entire tone of the lifelong relationship you will have with your beautiful little person. Love your children as they are; prove to them that they are enough as they are. Enjoy the pure, childlike unconditional love that comes flooding back.

Action Steps

1. Tell your children you love them, that you will always love them no matter what they do, and that you are proud to be their Mom/Dad.*

2. Hug your children as often as possible. Children need physical attention. Physical touch is an important way to show your unconditional love so they feel it.

*Try to make at least one of the action steps in this book a parenting habit. Learning is not enough, as nothing will change unless you actually make a commitment to do something different.

- These habits are designed so that they are simple, easy, and free, but they will have enormous future implications for your children and potentially your grandchildren.

- *Your strategy with any of these action steps should be to pick ONE STEP and do it every day for at least a month because it takes about 26 to 28 days of repeated action to create a habit.*

- *Any one of these steps will have a profound effect on your child's development.*

- *Create a small but powerful new habit every month or so, but try to take it one habit at a time.*

- *Habit change requires some daily focus as you make the new behavior part of your regular routine.*

- *Take it slow, leave this book lying around somewhere where you'll notice it from time to time, and revisit it on occasion when the calendar turns and it's time to move forward another small step on the journey of positive parental influence —your life's work.*

Use the space below as a reminder of what you need to do to put your steps into action:

Chapter One

Chapter Two

"All advancement in society begins with the development of the character of the young."

~ Aristotle

FOCUS ON TRANSFERRABLE SKILLS

Often well meaning parents focus on results as they try to encourage their children in a positive way following practices or games, instead of using this valuable feedback opportunity to focus on transferrable skills. Focusing on a consistent *approach* to the game will develop a child's character and reinforce an approach that can transfer successfully to other activities. This approach is also essential to a child's future success if he or she is to move into the upper echelons of the sport currently played.

Sport becomes a reference activity, a training ground to learn HOW to succeed; it reinforces an approach that will lead to long term success in any future endeavor. Parents should encourage transferrable attributes and skills like hard work, listening, diligence, enthusiasm, persistence, or the effective use of skills developed through earlier work (preparation). Again, this is just a subtle adjustment in coaching technique, but it will pay huge dividends in the child's development. It will teach the child an approach that will ensure enjoyment of the highest probability of success possible, both inside and outside the sport environment.

In 1996 and 1997, I played with a terrific future coach named Mark Dixon. Mark was a bright, funny guy and an outstanding athlete. He was one of a half-dozen people in the history of US sport to be a high school All American in one sport, and a college All American in a second sport. He went on to play for the Miami Dolphins for seven years until chronic back and ankle injuries ended his athletic career. We were teammates and roommates, and Mark influenced my career more than anyone because I never met anyone who was so obsessed with excellence. He was the most "approach oriented" player I had ever met. He was a huge believer in "success habits," fully understanding that research indicates that we are 96% to 98% habitual.

The following is Mark's favorite quote. He used to say it almost every day. Seeing the importance in it, I too memorized the words, and it too came to define the rest of my career as it did his:

> *"We are what we repeatedly do.*
> *Excellence, then, is not an act but a habit."*
> ~ Aristotle

Mark taught me to set a goal to get better each and every day, then create conscious routines that would lead to excellence. We worked together to improve our skills every time we had a break in practice. We built little routines that addressed fundamentals that were key to our success on the field. In addition, we would choose a daily or weekly "focus skill" that we would deliberately improve. I used that approach for the rest of my career, and taught it to several players who have since achieved all-star status. I am more proud of my over 2,000 consecutive "improvement" practices than I am of my Grey Cup championships, or my numerous all star seasons.

As Cervantes said, "The journey is better than the inn", and for me, the approach I learned (and now teach my children) is more valuable and more personally rewarding than any of the results I received through sport. I use this approach in every area of my life. Like most of the life skills I learned through organized sport, it is 100% transferrable.

FIND TRANSFERRABLE SKILLS TO REINFORCE DAILY

Positive reinforcement is the key to a healthy outlook. Children, like most parents, live in a world filled with negativity. Academic research indicates that the majority of an individual's daily thoughts in western culture are negative.

Your job when you watch practice or games, is to catch your child doing something well and reinforce it. Your child should feel great after your coaching. Validate the approach. Program your child to think positive thoughts so he or she will become a powerful, mentally tough, resilient adult.

"People will forget what you said, people will forget what you did,
but people will never forget how you made them feel."
~ Maya Angelou

This level of coaching diligence does necessitate some parental self-discipline. Many parents, when they find the time to attend practice, spend the entire time conversing with others, texting, emailing, or generally tuned out from their child's developmental experience. When parents attend games they often become results-oriented and allow their current emotions, not their long term parenting goals, to influence their evaluation of their child's performance. Then they unknowingly damage their child's mental skill development with post game or practice comments that are superficial, results oriented, or critical.

One day, while driving to work, I listened to the great parenting researchers Linda and Richard Eyre speak about "the most important minute of the day" in a relationship. When they asked what it was, I paused the CD and thought about it for a minute or two. I guessed that maybe it was the last minute before a husband and wife went to bed. When I started the CD again, I learned that, according to these two world-renowned social scientists, the most important minute in a married couple's life is the minute they see each other after work. By learning to drop their current mental agenda and focus in on each other's emotional needs for *just ONE minute,* a positive relationship tone for the entire evening gets established. The Eyres indicate that habitually repeating this pattern daily helps sustain a long-term happy marriage.

In a similar manner, I believe that sport parents can transform the entire sport experience for their child by dropping their agenda for *just ONE minute* after practices and games.

Take a minute after every practice and game and look your child right in the eye and focus on their emotional need for positive, approach-oriented feedback, even if your feedback is often repetitive. If you get this done in less than a minute, take a few seconds to thank the volunteer coaches who are helping you raise a hard working, high character team-oriented kid. The organized sport experience can be special, fun, nurturing, transferrable, bonding, and it can create a future winner out of your child . . . all by getting that one situation right. Not a bad return for a minute's work!

Positive reinforcement is easy when you consider how much your children want to please you and how much they enjoy repetition. I consistently tell my six year old son Sam that I am proud of how well he listens to his coaches and how hard he works (because both are true). One day I was preoccupied and quite frankly, tired of saying the same things over and over, and I neglected to mention these little comments after practice. I was still positive and cheerful, and I joked around with my little buddy, and bought him a post-workout gumball. We were halfway home when between chews I was asked the following reflective question from the back seat, "Dad, did I work hard today?". It surprised me how even the smallest repetitive comments can be important to your child, especially since he would often say, "I know that", or "You always say that". It's very important to do this simple task. You're the life coach. Your child just spent an hour doing his or her work — take a minute or two and do yours.

Parents, you MUST realize how important your daily influence is so PAY ATTENTION to your child's approach, attitude and progress during games and practices. Carefully think about what you will reinforce. Remember Gottman's "magic ratio". You are the most important influence, the life coach, the advisor. Your job is to guide your children in this world. Your discipline and attention to detail will define, in the child's mind, what the entire practice or game experience meant, and what the results really were. Incredibly, all this happens with just a well-placed comment or two. The key, of course, is repetition. Your discipline in this endeavor, over a number of years, will directly translate into their long-term approach to sport and life.

"It's amazing what you can see if you look."
~ Yogi Berra

I love watching my children practice. I do socialize a little, and I always try to be polite and kind to the other parents, but the truth is I am a family man through and through, and I absolutely love watching my children work and learn and strive and laugh. I don't care if I have to start work at 4 a.m. if that's what it takes to be present when they play organized sport. I feel like I understand what Plato meant when he said, "You can discover more about people in an hour of play than you can in a year of conversation."

I see my children and their friends learn, and change, and grow, and develop new skills — and this "paying attention" is what constantly reminds me that the window of time where my children will be young is far too small. I wouldn't miss a second of it for the world.

Small Daily Comments, Big Lasting Results

Remember, your long term GOAL is to develop your child in the best manner possible — to be the best he or she can be as a person, first and foremost. Develop someone during the formative years that you can be proud of the rest of your life. Parenting is so unlike any other job in the world — you do it for life. It doesn't stop when your child turns eighteen, although sometimes you might jokingly wish for such. You will be a parent until you die. Put the time and effort in during the first ten or twelve years, and don't prioritize urgent things over important things. Get to as many practices and games as possible; be punctual about it; take it seriously, and pay attention to your child out there. Look for positive behaviors to reinforce. Be diligent about coaching your child to have great character through the sport experience. Start right away, and do it every practice or game until your child becomes a self-sufficient adult.

There is a terrific organization in the US called the Positive Coaching Alliance that has created some helpful tools to assist parents and coaches. The founder is Jim Thompson (Stanford University) and their National Advisory Board is made up of coaching legends, great former professional athletes and Olympians, and highly respected sport and child psychologists. Their mission is to "transform youth sports so youth sports can transform youths". They seek to "transform the culture of youth sports to give all young athletes the opportunity for a positive, character-building experience." This group of experts believes that positive reinforcement and never losing focus on the goal of character development are the keys to transforming youth through organized sport. Before dismissing this as indulgent pandering, remember this is no group of softies — these are hardcore experts, many of whom have had Hall of Fame careers, or who won multiple world championships, or Gold medals; they are dedicated academics who have spent years doing first class research on children and children's development.

> *"How wonderful it is that nobody need wait a single moment before starting to improve the world."*
> ~ Anne Frank

Done well, positive parenting is SUPER FUN and SUPER REWARDING. Dr. Steven Covey once observed that when you parent your children, you actually parent your grandchildren. The lever of influence you have during those ten years is incredibly long.

Think about all the wonderful things a high character, great leader could accomplish in the world. . .

- *Do everything you can to reinforce great character in your child.*

- *Do your part to re-establish the character ethic in your community.*

- *Influence one of tomorrow's great people, maybe even one of tomorrow's great leaders.*

- *Use sport to teach your child how to succeed at any endeavor.*

- *Set a goal to focus on transferrable skills during the years your child participates in sport.*

- *Have a terrific time raising your very own little winner!*

DEVELOP YOUR CHILD'S SELF-DISCIPLINE

The most important characteristic a parent can develop in a child is self-discipline. Inner-directed people are always more competent and successful than outer-directed people. Fifty years ago author and self-development guru Napoleon Hill spent twenty years studying the wealthiest and most successful businesspeople in the world and concluded that self-discipline was the "master key to success". Self-discipline can be defined as doing what you should do whether you feel like it or not. Self-discipline is directly correlated with self-esteem, which is "your reputation with yourself".

Self-discipline is easily developed through organized sport. The approach for children is simple:

1. Children must learn to experiment fearlessly with the myriad of life choices available to them. When they choose a sport for the first time, they should be allowed to quit if it doesn't suit them. When they choose to participate in a sport the second time,

encourage them not to quit, or miss practice except for illness or some other very important reason.

Ensure you help your child think his or her commitment through before making it, and he or she will learn about resolve and dependability. You can even frame this approach as a family value, for example, "In this family we don't quit things we have committed to," or "In this family we don't let our teammates down."

2.   Children have two clear goals every practice. Their goals are to get a tiny bit better and to have fun.

Your approach to developing your own self-discipline through your supportive role in the organized sport experience is also simple:

1.   *Prioritize your time so you can attend as many practices and games as possible.*

2.   *Stay focused on verbally supporting your child's goals for the training session — to get a little better and have fun. Talk about these goals before practice and then reinforce them after practice.*

3.   *Verbally support your child after the training session by commenting on areas of improvement you noted, fun moments you witnessed, etc. Show that your child's behaviour is important enough for you to pay attention. Repeat this to your child like a mantra, "I'm going to watch your every move out there because you're so important!"*

4. *Avoid commenting on results like goals, wins, etc. except to frame the comment in a way that supports the approach you are teaching the child. For example, you can state, "You scored a nice goal — your hard work every day is really paying off!" or "Great win today; your team is getting a little better every practice and it's really starting to show!" Your work is to focus on your child's approach — results, like goals, touchdowns, wins, etc. are rewarding enough for the child without your input.*

5. *Repeatedly mention the benefits of listening and working hard, and praise progress in either of these areas every chance you get.*

6. *Have fun and enjoy your little person and their exciting journey through the challenges and drama of organized sport.*

7. *Try to positively influence all children, not just your own. Take the broad view that we're all in this together, and that we can make a positive difference in each other's lives by helping each other raise successful children.*

Carol Dweck of Stanford University (and a member of the Positive Coaching Alliance National Advisory Board) authored a book entitled *Mindset: The New Psychology of Success.* In this book she identifies two mindsets that play an enormous role in creating optimal performance and determining long-term success.

The first mindset is the "fixed" mindset — this entails a belief that an individual has a fixed amount of athletic talent, or intellectual talent, or musical talent.

The second mindset is the "growth" mindset — this entails a belief that an individual can grow and improve no matter where he or she starts.

One of Dweck's fascinating findings is that when adults praise children for their TALENT instead of their approach, they actually DEMOTIVATE their children over time. Children fear challenges that may compromise the TALENT LABEL they have been given. They fear losing their reputation for being "smart" or "athletic" or "musical". Alternatively, when children get praised for their effort or their diligence or their self-discipline they reinforce these wonderful labels by committing to the process that ensures their continued growth — this process is often called "deliberate practice", which basically means focused daily work.

As a parent, you WILL influence your child's mindset. If you choose to believe your child has a "fixed amount" of talent, and pass that limiting belief on to your child, you will do tremendous damage to your child's ability to create and attain ambitious hopes and dreams. You will negate the desire to create self-discipline, you will erode the importance of hard work, and you will disable your child's ability to persist through adversity. In addition, you will perpetuate a destructive MYTH.

I find it very easy to teach this important mindset to my children, and not only because I was a terrible football player before I was a very good one. I was lousy at most things I tried, whether it was walking, running, spelling my name, learning to skate, hit a baseball . . . you get the picture. Make it a habit to remind your children that "all masters were once disasters".

My son played his first "real" hockey game the other day, and he asked me twice in the hours leading up to the game, "Dad, what if we lose?" (imagine a 6 year old concerned about losing — it's hard to believe, but these events are big to these little people). I told him I lost almost every game my first year playing football, and by the end of my career we won almost every game. Surely you have similar stories of early struggles, early losses, and later improvements. It doesn't matter if you were 5 or 35 when the reputed events occurred; teach your child about your growth, not your talent. Be sure to share your struggles and you improvements with your child. Developing a "growth mindset" is easy and it's a critical step if you want your child to fully develop his or her talents.

As I mentioned, I went from one of the worst college football players in Canada to one of the best professional football players in Canada in less than ten years. Here are a few other success stories of athletes who refused to limit their mindset:

My friend **Al MacInnis** became an NHL Hall of Famer after he was moved from forward to defense in Junior hockey because he was reputedly too slow to make it as a forward.

Michael Jordan became (arguably) the greatest basketball player in history after getting cut from his high school basketball team.

Mia Hamm was born with a club foot and had to wear corrective shoes as a toddler. She went on to become one of the greatest female soccer players ever and was named FIFA World Player of the Year twice.

Tom Brady became one of the best quarterbacks in NFL history as a 6th round draft pick.

Undrafted **Martin St Louis** became the 2004 NHL scoring champ.

Wilma Rudolph fought polio as a child and doctors told her she would never walk again. She fought her weakness for years, and became the fastest woman in the world in the 1960's and a three time gold medalist.

James Harrison was cut in four NFL training camps prior to becoming the 2008 NFL defensive player of the year.

There is no such thing as a "fixed" amount of talent. Give your kid a break.

In my late twenties and thirties, I've had players (and often ones I've personally mentored) surpass my on field abilities at the pro level. Development takes place in different ways, at different times, for athletes.

Teach your children that "sport performance and achievement" is a marathon, not a sprint.

People "blossom" at different times, and often in unexpected ways. It could happen anytime in the next couple of decades, or it could happen in a completely different sport or endeavor. Never make the amateurish mistake of trying to judge talent at the youth sports level. Even professional scouts and general managers struggle to figure out how good a kid is going to be, and they're certainly not trying to make these predictions when a child is six, eight, or ten years of age.

Remember when your pediatrician warned you that all children walk at different ages, talk at different ages, and develop social skills at different ages? And that none of these timelines were predictive of their long term competence in that area? All children develop at different ages and in different ways. When I was a youngster my aunt, who has a Master's degree in early childhood development, took my mother aside and asked her if I was "slow" mentally (my brothers and sisters love that story!). In terms of physical development, I grew to an adult height of 6'5" despite being 5'9" heading into high school. I was still growing taller my first year of university. I can't help but laugh when I hear parents "evaluating" the talent limitations of youth athletes. Dr John Gray put it this way:

> "Children are different in the way they learn. It is essential for parents to understand this difference, otherwise they may begin comparing children and become unnecessarily frustrated. When it comes to learning a task, there are three kinds of children: runners, walkers, and jumpers. Runners learn very quickly. Walkers learn in a

steady manner and give clear feedback that they are making steady progress. Finally, there are the jumpers. Jumpers tend to be more difficult to raise. They don't seem to be learning anything or making any progress, and then one day they make one jump and have it. Jumpers are like late bloomers. Learning takes more time for them."

Just enjoy being supportive. Do yourself, and all the other kids, coaches and parents a favor and drop the "talent evaluator" title from your resume.

Believe in the incredible, amazing stories that get created all the time in the real world. Teach your children that they can do anything they put their mind to if they are willing to pay the price. Self-discipline, hard work, persistence, courage, faith and a little support along the way is the magic elixir that creates long term, lasting success. Big, exciting success stories are created every day, and they can happen for your child too, either in the activity they are involved in or one that is completely unrelated. They will eventually find something they love and that they're great at, and if you believe in them they will learn to believe in themselves.

Action Steps

- *Always focus on the child's approach, not their short term results or "talent".*

- *Catch them doing something right, whether it's working hard at practice, using good manners, smiling or laughing, or being nice to their friends.*

- *Reinforce that behavior with a sincere compliment.*

- *Treat your child's development like it's a marathon, not a sprint.*

Use the space below to record skills you struggled with and then mastered, and then share those experiences with your child so they develop a "growth mindset".

_____

_____

_____

_____

_____

_____

_____

_____

Chapter Three

"It is easier to build strong children than to repair broken men."

~ Frederick Douglass

EXPECTATIONS

Just as you get what you expect from yourself, you get what you expect from your child.

There have been hundreds of double-blind studies done in recent decades that confirm "social expectation theory". Many have been done using teachers and students in schools.

Basically, these studies are most often designed so that they are double-blind — meaning that neither the students nor the teachers know that they are involved in a study. Usually the researchers tell the teachers they are exceptional (which may or may not be true) and they tell the teachers that the students they are about to teach are exceptional (which is not true). The teachers then spend a period of time teaching the students, and researchers always find that the expectations of the teachers have an enormous effect on the results experienced by the students.

The students excel and get impressive results because the teachers get the results they expect. Conversely, when teachers expect poor results because of prior beliefs about their own competencies or the competencies of their students, they get poor results. Expectations play an enormous role in the determination of results. There have been hundreds of these types of double-blind studies done all over the world and the results are irrefutable . . . expectations matter.

SET HIGH EXPECTATIONS FOR YOURSELF AND YOUR CHILD

"High expectations are the key to everything."
~ Sam Walton

How should "social expectation theory" influence you as a sports parent?

1. *First, you should believe in your own competence as an influential, effective teacher and role model for your child.*

2. *Second, you should believe your child is exceptional, and will do wonderful, positive things in the world. In other words, you should have high expectations, and consequently high standards, for both yourself and your child.*

3. *Third, you should believe it's unlikely you have found the one thing that your child is here to do best. There*

are over 50,000 different job titles in North America, and your child is just starting to reveal her interests and strengths.

4. *Fourth, sport can be an excellent way to teach your child how to develop excellence when she does discover what she wants to do with her life.*

5. *Fifth, ensure your expectations are about the child's approach, and NOT about the child's results (or future as a professional athlete or on the podium).*

6. *Sixth, always remember that success as an athlete and success in any other endeavor require similar mental, social, and emotional programming because all great teams want great people. Stay focused on the long-term "expectation" of creating a high character person by teaching a "growth mindset", using the "magic ratio" to fill your child's "emotional tank", and by modeling a strong work ethic, great interpersonal skills, and a commitment to continuous personal growth yourself.*

"Whatever you are, be a good one."
~ Abraham Lincoln

One of the reasons expectations are so important is because they tie directly into what the parent, as a primary influence in the child's life, believes is possible (or probable) for the child. This in turn influences what the child believes is possible for him or herself. Self-belief is a big,

big deal in sport and life. In fact, without self-belief, there is no chance of succeeding as an athlete or as a leader.

> *"It's lack of faith that makes people afraid of meeting challenges, and I believed in myself."*
> ~ Muhammad Ali

When I was a young athlete training to compete at the University level, future NHL Hall of Famer, Stanley Cup Champion, and Norris Trophy winner Al McInnis mentored me with a simple one-on-one conversation about belief. Al was from the same tiny home town as me (Port Hood, Nova Scotia), and one day, years before I played professional football, he told me that in his opinion, non-belief was the single most difficult challenge for young athletes to overcome. He said you have to believe in yourself, and you have to hang onto that belief through all the setbacks, and all the inevitable disappointments, but even more importantly, through all the negative criticism and doubts expressed by others about your ability to excel at your sport and fulfill your dreams.

My own experiences through the next eighteen years of organized sport at the amateur and professional level mirrored the validity of Al's statement. You have to believe you can grow to accomplish great things. You have to believe in your own potential, and the true test of that belief is whether you will do the work day-in, day-out, even if it feels like your goals are beyond your current abilities.

> *"If you treat a person as he is, he will stay as he is.*
> *But if you treat him as if he were what he ought to be,*
> *he will become that bigger and better person."*
> ~ Johann von Goethe

Self-belief is of critical importance, and without it the athlete is doomed to fail.

As a parent, it is necessary to maintain a healthy dose of confidence in the child's ability to excel at anything they work passionately toward. Who cares if the parent errs on the side of being overly positive or overly optimistic? It's so much worse to be critical, to dampen their spirit, erode their confidence, and to weaken their resolve. Children need support while they take personal responsibility for their approach and their results, and they need to learn to hang onto their long-term goals through the inevitable setbacks and adversity that are part of the journey to excellence.

Choose to be your child's #1 supporter. Believe in your child's potential to be great at something. The world can be a cold, hard, unforgiving place at times, especially if you strive to do great things. Be their ally in life, their #1 fan, the rock they lean on for support while they build their own beliefs, their own expectations, and thus their own resolve, their own courage, and their own faith.

Action Steps

1. *Tell your children you have high expectations for them because they're special.*

2. *Say "That might be OK for others, but you're my daughter/ son, and I know how special and important you are, and I know what you're capable of . . . that's why I expect more from you."*

3. *Expect more from yourself as a teacher and role model.*

4. *Parenting is the most important work you'll ever do. Change one small parenting or role model habit today.*

5. *Make becoming a world-class parent a real priority in your life.*

6. *Teach your child to take responsibility for their approach and their results, and to never blame coaches or teammates.*

7. *Teach your child to "expect" the journey to excellence to be long, challenging, and, if they are passionate about it, totally worth all the effort, struggle, and heartbreak!*

Record your expectations here both for yourself and your child so that you might revisit them.

_____

_____

_____

Chapter Four

"A child seldom needs a good talking to as a good listening to."

~ Robert Brault

PATIENCE

We live in an instant world — instant food, instant weight loss, instant wealth, instant everything. Most of what we are promised is marketing garbage designed to prey on our insatiable appetite for fast, easy, effortless results. The quick and easy approach to meaningful results is almost always a trap. This approach generally leads to a pattern of short-term change that is unsustainable, and then a regression to our prior state, or worse yet, one with even less confidence and self-belief.

Advertising has been a huge, insidious influence on our culture for decades, and often these brilliant, professional marketers know more about our psychology and emotional desires and fears than we do. And they know all about the power of repetition as well. Most research findings indicate that we are influenced by THOUSANDS of advertising messages every day!

- *Please don't think you have not been affected by advertising.*

- *Pay attention for an hour or so, and you'll start to see advertising everywhere.*

- *Pay special attention to the amount of outrageous, "instant results with almost no effort" advertising.*

"The two most powerful warriors are patience and time."
~ Leo Tolstoy

Our ancestors knew better. They would be shocked by modern advertising, as it would contradict many of the basic universal laws they experienced in nature every day. Generally things change a little every day, and in time those changes are massive. Being part of nature, we exhibit similar tendencies.

You reap what you sow, and often the role nature takes in that process is excruciatingly slow. It takes years of daily improvement to achieve mastery in a discipline, whether it is a sport, a traditional career, occupation, or a business.

The "get-rich-quick, become an overnight success" stuff gets you killed financially 99 times out of 100, and the only one who tends to get rich is the one who sold you on the idea.

"Lose thirty pounds in six weeks" or "rock solid abs by spring" advertising is the norm as advertisers try to trump each other's promises to get past the noise. Unless you have been living under a rock you have been influenced by these messages that often contradict any common sense analysis about what goal achievement really takes.

Most studies on mastery, whether in or outside of sport, support the 10,000 hours over ten years theory first postulated by Dr. Anders Ericsson. His work, which dealt mainly with musical and athletic excellence, suggests that you have to put the time in to develop mastery on a day-by-day basis for at least ten years, and that you cannot speed the process up by working 20,000 hours over five years. You have to plug away steadily at something he called "deliberate practice" for almost three hours a day for about a decade if you want to achieve mastery. Deliberate practice is hard work — it is practicing on the edge of your current abilities, so you are growing and changing and improving. It is not just showing up and coasting along, and it requires significant rest and recovery as well.

My football experiences, and the experiences of a lot of former athletes in my personal network, support this approach. Like many athletes, I was conditioned to believe in constant daily improvement.

Even after each six month season of six day per week training in the Canadian Football League, I preferred to forsake extended rest, and usually began off-season training within a few days after the previous season ended. I wanted to improve constantly, and even if I was fatigued from the previous season there were always little things I could do to get better — like flexibility work, technique work, film study, or joint-friendly core training. My favorite off-season training quote was a Baltazar Gracian quote that stated, "Time and I against any other two." I felt I was competing against my opponents every day of the off-season, and I wanted to win that one-on-one battle of will and desire.

I felt I just had to do something to get better or the day was wasted and I wouldn't get it back. Then when my deeper energy stores came back, I would be much farther ahead than if I had taken several weeks off, which I also tried (once). This attitude is quite prevalent amongst high performing athletes. You can't waste your days, even if you just do something tiny to get better.

CHOOSE THE SLOW, STEADY, NO EXCUSES APPROACH

"I find the great thing in this world is not so much where we stand, as in what direction we are moving."
~ Oliver Wendell Holmes

Best to think like the tortoise, not the hare. Take the long sure road. Goal achievement takes focus, resolve, and patience. Our best chance to make our dreams come true is to doggedly move forward in that direction. It is important to remember the popular little truism, "The elevator to success is always out of order, but the stairs work every time."

Consistently take small steps forward in the direction of your goals.

"He that can have patience can have all things."
~ Benjamin Franklin

Build lasting success one step at a time, one day at a time. Build your character and your skills while you build your dreams. Great and lasting things are usually built slowly, whether it is your character, your leadership skills, your athletic skills, your reputation in business, or your net worth. Get on that road and stay on that road.

One of the toughest concepts to figure out is something I now see in success literature called the "Law of Accumulation".

This law suggests that (provided you have carefully thought through a proven approach) you stick with what you are doing, even if in the short-term, the results are discouraging. You run those stairs; you keep lifting those weights; you keep practicing those technical skills; you just keep fighting and scratching for that miserable inch of progress, even when it does not feel like anything positive is getting accomplished.

Your effort "accumulates" beneath the surface somewhere, and if you just keep working the results you seek will show up.

I had an old coach who used to call this "fighting through the freeze" and it meant pushing forward through perceived stalemates, and success ultimately went to those who did, and never to those who quit or made excuses and changed course.

- **Al MacInnis** developed the hardest slap shot in the world by taking hundreds of shots daily against the brick exterior of the Port Hood School. No fancy facilities, no excuses. Just hard work and daily improvements too small to measure. Later in his career, Al trained under successful Olympic coach Charles Poliquin, working hard for hours each week, with the goal of adding one mile (less than 1%) per hour on his slap shot each year.

- **Larry Bird** shot 500 free throws each day before getting on the school bus every weekday morning in French Lick, Indiana. After joining the Boston Celtics and deciding he wanted to add a fade away jump shot to his game, Larry added an additional 90 minutes to his already grueling off-season routine, taking 800 fade away jump shots per day.

- **Wayne Gretzky** begged his father Walter to take him to the park every day to practice hockey for as much as three hours per day. Walter eventually tired of the cold and built his infamous backyard rink so he could watch his son from the warmth of his kitchen. Wayne practiced for several hours every day as a child and their little rink was in constant use from noon until ten p.m. every day.

- **None** of these successful athletes demanded, or received, instant results. They took the slow, sure, steady approach. They put the work in daily and got the results they earned.

* **None** of these athletes were taught disempowering excuses by their parents. Early struggles were never the coach's fault, or a teammates fault or a lack of facilities or a lack of support or some other silly story that eroded the athlete's ability to take personal responsibility for their own long term development and ultimately, their own success.

Athletes cannot make excuses and take personal responsibility at the same time. Excuses are often just stories that emphasize conditions outside of the athlete's control, and thus they "excuse" the athlete from working on the things he or she can control. That's why at the professional level, excuses are "off limits". Great coaches despise excuses. Excuses destroy initiative. They absolve the athlete of the necessity of an improved course of action that will eventually lead to better results.

Are you one of those parents that "supports" your child's development in organized sport by blaming coaches or other outside circumstances? Do you "encourage" your child by making excuses for him or her?

If so, you are their #1 obstacle on their "success journey" in sport and life. *You are teaching your young leader, by example, that it's OK to make excuses and to blame others for their results. Even if you're right you're wrong. Let it go. Whatever the "big, dramatic, emotional, damaging circumstance or decision"* *is, it is just one setback, one issue, one relationship, or even one season. You will teach your child more by remaining focused on long-term objectives and by taking the high road than you ever will by confronting a coach or teammate or other parent about a perceived issue with your child's playing time or development, unless the behavior in question is unethical or verbally or physically abusive.*

Remain focused on doing your job as a guide and influential leader in your child's life, and use whatever adversity sport has presented your child as a "character teaching" moment. Remember the ABC rule — Adversity Builds Character . . . but only if you, the child's guide, frame the event correctly, because the RESPONSE to adversity is what actually builds character, not the adversity itself. Your child's athletic and leadership development is a marathon, not a sprint. It is very important to teach your child a "no excuses" mentality by modeling one yourself. It's not always easy, but I bet you can do it if you really try.

Instead, teach your child the mantra of the personally responsible champion, which is, **"What can I do to improve the results I'm getting?"**

If you can't discipline yourself to take this small but CRITICAL step, you would do your child a favor by sending them to practices and games with a friend and staying out of the sport scene altogether. You will doom your child to failure at the elite levels of their sport, and because taking personal responsibility for results is SO IMPORTANT to life success, you will have wasted a significant portion of the transferrable benefits of your organized sport investment. Your child will learn more on their own through the sport experience than they will with your "support" if you teach your child to blame others and make excuses during difficult times.

"You're not a failure until you start to blame."
~ John Wooden

An astute friend who spent decades in high performance soccer and then raised some very successful student athletes told this story about how they, as parents, chose to handle their "invitation to show support by blaming others" when their children were young:

"When playing time became an issue, kids would often get in the car and question why they didn't play as much as 'Sally' did. Usually athletes know where they are in the 'pecking order' (for lack of a better phrase) and they know why they didn't play as much as some of the more skilled players, but they'd want to hear Mom and Dad's thoughts on the matter.

In our youth soccer experience, some parents innocently told their young player that she was just as good if not better than 'Sally' and that she most certainly should have played just as much. This often did a huge disservice to both their daughter and to teammate Sally. Now their daughter felt powerless to change her results, and Sally was perceived as an overrated player instead of as a successful teammate and role model. The daughter was given, by her influential life mentors, the right to blame both Sally and the coaching staff for her results.

These parents thought they were supporting their daughter, but the truth was they were enabling disastrous mental programming. They created a false sense of entitlement. They created a disempowering separation between "approach" and "results" in the child's mind.

Our kids have spent time on the bench and they have asked us the exact same questions. As tempting as it was to make them feel better and tell them it's not their fault, we instead directed a few questions their way:

- Why do you think you did not play as much?

- What could you work on so that you won't be denied field time?

- Are you willing to spend extra time on developing those skills?

They usually knew all the answers. If they were unsure we directed them toward their coach to ask, 'What do I need to work on in order to get on the field more'?

This approach worked really well for us, and besides making every season much more enjoyable, we feel it has helped our children learn to take responsibility for their own results in other areas of their lives as well."

Learn to think like successful people by reading their biographies. You'll find that their success was almost always a long, drawn out process with lots of trying times and moments of doubt. You'll see the same basic pattern over and over. All athletes face difficult times and difficult people, and they work through and past these obstacles and issues, and actually grow and become stronger BECAUSE of them. Difficult situations are an important part of the growth process. In these biographies you won't find excuses, and you won't find a short, fast, easy journey to the top. You will read about personal responsibility and hard work. You'll feel a lot better about your own struggles to succeed, and you'll do a better job preparing your children for the long road of daily improvement ahead.

I remember reading about Michael Jordan crying on the bus after they lost to the Detroit Pistons yet again in the playoffs. It made me feel better when I lost my second consecutive Grey Cup game — a heart breaker in front of 65,000 of our own fans in my 9th year in the CFL.

The pain of losing a championship does not last for a day or two; it can last for months or even years. It is hard to shake the disappointment of a missed opportunity that might never arrive again. I remember one of my best friends asking me a couple of months later if I suffered a concussion in the game. Apparently I wasn't quite myself.

In the meantime, I kept working, kept pushing, kept fighting for that daily inch. I knew from the stories I'd read in books and watched on TV that champions are tough. They keep plugging despite short term setbacks. Champions don't make excuses about anything, including teammates, coaches, field conditions, injuries, or other outside circumstances. They get to work. They get better. Champions never let how they feel interfere with what they have to do. There's a big difference between suffering a defeat and being defeated, no matter how the loss feels at the time. I knew winners used the pain as fuel to work even harder. I'd watched my friend Al MacInnis win the Stanley Cup with the Calgary Flames in 1989 after some painful losses to the Edmonton Oiler dynasty in the 1980's. Jordan won six NBA titles after those heartbreaking playoff losses to the Pistons, and my team won our next two Grey Cup appearances against the very team that had beat us in that agonizing loss on our home field in 2002. Winning is so sweet after those difficult defeats and all that work.

Biographies often breathe new life into old words like discipline, character, resolve, persistence, courage and integrity. If you pick up a sports biography, you'll also stumble across adversities and vices like jealousy, spite, and resentment from peers and competitors, especially in the early years. Nothing you experience, either positive or negative, will be brand new to society. Someone went through it, handled it, and wrote about it. Learn from their experiences.

Successful people generally overcome a lot to be successful, regardless of their field of endeavor. Expect to endure some adversity as you strive to get the results you deserve. Never make excuses or blame others. A strong, steady determination to move forward despite short term setbacks always characterizes the lives of successful people.

"I am a slow walker, but I never walk back."
~ Abraham Lincoln

Parents:

- *Stop demanding instant results. Mastery is a 10,000 hour, ten year journey.*

- *Never blame others or make excuses for your child's progress.*

- *Take a day by day, sustained, patient approach to eventually getting positive results.*

- *Stay focused on your long-term goal to raise a great kid first, a "winning athlete" second. The two go hand in hand anyway.*

"The only way a kid is going to practice is if it's total fun for him. . . and it was for me!"
~ Wayne Gretzky

I loved practice. My favorite part of football was getting better at it daily. I didn't grow up in an area that offered organized football, but whenever we would play it after school, I would play until everyone went home. In college I would be so jacked up after practice it would take me a couple of hours to come down.

At the professional level, I liked practice even better than game day, although I loved walking into the locker room after a win, hugging my teammates, feeling really great about what we accomplished, and feeling great about having done my very best — having really put it on the line for three hours.

Despite the joy of winning, practice was the best for me — the work, the fun, the sunshine and green grass, the joking around, the joyful little competitions with teammates. I thought this was unusual until I found some convincing academic research by Dr Luc Pellitier. His findings indicate that a very strong predictor of long-term athletic excellence is when athletes say they "practice sport to experience pleasure". This research completely resonated with my sport experience — I enjoyed practice a great deal.

Learning the importance of "learning to love the practice process" has also immediately impacted how I support my children in organized sport. I teach my children this important principle:

"Kids who learn to love practice are likely to become great at what they do."

If our children decide they want to become great at their chosen sport, or hobby, or interest, then we should teach them to learn to love practicing it a little every day.

It is so easy to teach this important principle. Every time I catch my children practicing, whether it is piano, hockey, soccer, reading, writing, drawing or other work, I compliment them on their approach, and remind them that that is how everyone who became great at anything did it. If we choose not to teach our children this simple truism, we are ignoring one of the fundamental tenants to success in any aspect of life: practice makes you better. If they enjoy practice, they'll continue to practice.

We are not telling them to become great, or that they have to, or that we want them to; we are simply teaching them, with the kind of clarity a five, or seven, or nine year old can understand, exactly HOW to become great at any complex skill IF THEY WANT TO.

If choosing to enjoy practice is such an important predictor of future excellence, and how a child views practice is a choice very much influenced by the parent, then the loving, supportive, encouraging parent needs do their best to make practice rewarding and enjoyable. This effort on your part could help your child become excellent at a chosen endeavor more than anything else you read in this book.

I have to add this caveat though . . . you can make it fun, you can be supportive, but in the end your child, not you, determines how he or she feels about the activity.

Currently, at the time of writing this book, my son is six, and like many of his friends, he's a nifty little hockey player. One day we were late for practice and I was stressed out and late trying to get him to practice on time, hustling along like a typical busy sports parent.

When I played sports, I hated being late for practice, and I was so obsessive about being prepared for games that I would go to the locker room four hours before the game started. You read correctly — four hours ahead.

Naturally I assumed Sam would be just like me, excited and determined to get to work, but no, he wasn't. My tousled-haired son was in the back seat happily chewing gum. "Don't worry about being late, Dad." He said, "I like it."

I said, "What do you mean you like it, Sam?"

He said, "I like being late. It's shorter that way."

I laughed so hard. Kids are great. They cut right to the truth. He might never have the same desire, the same drive, the same obsessive love of practice that I had (or he might develop it later), and that's more than OK. He's my favorite little boy of all time. I couldn't love him anymore than I do, and I thank God every day for my special little friend. I want to help him, support him, love him, and guide him, and when he does find something he's completely passionate about, his youth sport background will ensure he knows exactly how to become excellent at it. That's my "sports parent" approach and I'm sticking to it.

Build your Child's Character Slowly over Time

Building the self-esteem, character, and leadership skills of children is a slow, day by day practice. We need to start early with that goal in mind, and then stay the course consistently, day in and day out. We must never lose sight of our long term goal. As sports parents our goal is to develop children of high character, and our determination to use every possible practice and game experience over a decade or so to achieve that goal will manifest the results we expect. Remember the "long time perspective" findings of Dr Edward Banfield of Harvard University — you will successfully raise a high character, positive winner if you remain committed to that long term goal.

"Patience and fortitude conquer all things."
~ Ralph Waldo Emerson

Unconditional love affirmed regularly, positive encouragement, communication about their life, their challenges, their interests . . . all these things must happen on a day to day basis if we are to shape our child's character and leadership skills.

We must enjoy our time as guides and mentors, and learn to savor the sweet joy of the most important job we will ever have. We need to take the slow, consistent approach with high standards and a clear long term goal.

- *Imagine helping grow your child into a great leader that truly understands people and cares deeply about them.*

- *Imagine if your child learned to formulate a clear vision for his or her own life, and possibly even for others as well.*

- *Imagine your child having core values and learning to live them.*

- *Imagine your child having the skills and the courage to develop his or her "passionate purpose" in life.*

All these things are real possibilities, but often they take years of personal development, challenges, exposure to other people, successes, and failures. There are periods of joy and happiness punctuated by times of indecision, difficulty, adversity and angst. There is no short road to "knowing thyself". Maturing into a person with character, or an inspiring leader, takes time, and it takes periods of challenge, and periods of reflection.

The long journey through the minefield of short term results, often in the presence of equally challenged peers and supportive adults, is one of the reasons why sport, reinforced well, is such a great teacher.

I watch my children win and lose, succeed and fail, and there are lessons in each of those experiences. Amateur sport is a challenging, often emotional, educational experience. It is not all about winning. It is about what we learn when we try to win.

> **It is not all about winning. It is about what we learn when we try to win.**

It is easy to let emotions get in the way of the overall goal of youth sport — which should always be personal development. This is especially true on game day, when winning, or a child's individual contribution, can seem so important.

I was a competitor in sport for a long time, and I am sometimes vulnerable to strong competitive feelings when I watch my children play. Whenever I feel that emotional surge during games, I consciously think about the short term "competitive" trap those emotions lead to. I force myself to remember what my long-term goals are — to raise great kids, *and to help every other parent raise great kids too. Even if the parents, or the kids, are on the other team.*

Youth sport is not a competition; it is a collaboration ... and it is not just about sport; it is about life. We're all in it together, and we all want to raise great kids. We are raising a new generation of future adults. If we do our job well, these new people could change the world in wonderful ways. These "long time perspective" thoughts lead to sincere feelings of service, community and connection. They remove all the negativity from the sports scene; they change what I focus on, and they allow me to truly enjoy the whole amateur sports ride with all the other parents (even the crazy ones that yell insults at referees).

Families who truly understand the positive impact sport can have on youth are tremendous assets to their communities. I would never have become a successful football player were it not for the "sport values" of a family in my home community, Port Hood. I did not go to university to play football. I went to university to study Political Science. My friend Robert MacInnis, who had just finished his junior hockey career, went to Acadia as a freshman with me. We went to a football game together, and I made an offhand remark to Robert. I said, "I think I could play this game." Robert later convinced an assistant coach that I was worth recruiting because Robert was from a family that felt sport was extremely important, even transformational.

Robert has a persuasive, charismatic, almost pushy way of making things happen, and he managed to facilitate a meeting and then a try-out for me with the Acadia Axemen. Despite being a terrible football player, I made the team on potential alone, and my football career became the single most important educational experience of my life. I owe my start in football to Robert and his family's sport values, and for believing that I deserved a chance.

If you have these values, you can make a positive difference to some of the other kids in your sphere of influence as well. Don't be afraid to reach out and encourage not only your own kids, but other kids you come in daily contact with as well. All children can use a little extra support.

You will not be your children's only influence, but by taking an active daily role in their development, you can earn the right to be their most important influence even during the challenging teen years.

It is your duty to patiently guide your children through the formative process, patiently asking the right questions, taking an interest in their development, really listening and paying attention, and most importantly, leading by example as you strive to live your best life. It is an awesome responsibility, but our kids are definitely worth it!

Developing a life purpose, strong character, and effective leadership skills takes years of trial and error. We shouldn't expect it to happen quickly. It is better to take the slow, steady approach to this important work, and enjoy the journey.

Action Steps

1. *Ask your children questions and really listen to their answers.*

2. *Use meal time as an opportunity for conversation and connection.*

3. *Take an active interest, in their lives, **every day.***

4. *Read or watch biographies of people you respect to identify trends that will help you respond to challenges in your life.*

5. *Read or watch biographies of people you respect to identify trends that will help you respond to challenges in your child's life.*

6. *Teach your children to take personal responsibility for their lives by modeling a "no excuses" mentality.*

Lead by example. Please record excuses you make, or list people you blame, for some of the results you are getting in your life. Let those excuses go, and let the blame go. Ask, instead, what you can do to get different results in those areas so you are happier and more successful.

Chapter Five

"Children are unpredictable.
You never know what inconsistency they're going to catch you in next."

~ Franklin P. Jones

LEAD BY EXAMPLE

It is very difficult to raise a child with strong character if you display less than desirable character. Like all human beings, children have twenty-two times more nerve receptors running from their eyes to their brain than from their ears to their brain. Yet time after time parents say one thing and do another. As a parent, you are the child's most important role model, and kids do what their role models DO, not what they SAY. Ensuring that your words and your behavior don't contradict is extremely important.

Children are very astute and they know when the actions don't match the words, or when the actions are not exactly in the best interests of all parties, and inconsistency can lead to even more confusion as to what is or is not right. By far the most effective way to coach children is for parents to improve their own behavior.

Parents: Evaluate your daily choices by considering the following questions:

1. What am I thinking?

2. What am I eating?

3. What am I saying?

4. Do I exercise?

5. How are my relationship skills?

6. Do I gossip?

7. How do I treat my spouse or partner?

8. How do I treat my friends?

9. What do I watch on TV or the Internet?

10. How much time do I devote to TV or the Internet?

11. What do I read?

12. How do I conduct my own life?

13. Do I have goals?

14. Do I strive to improve my life and the lives of those around me?

15. Have I let my dreams die?

16. What do I think of the person in the mirror?

"Young people need models, not critics."
~ John Wooden

Often ill-informed parents and coaches who have not exercised or made healthy food choices in decades harp to kids about fitness, conditioning, or self-discipline. Parents and coaches who are incapable of controlling their emotions often try to coach kids about mental peak performance. Some parents criticize coaches without attending practice, learning about the game, studying practice or game video, or offering to help the program in any way. They do not realize the negative or adverse effects these actions can have on their children or the volunteers who coach the sport.

When I first went to play for the Eskimos back in 1998 my position coach was an old guy with a bad leg named Mike Bender. He became a hero of mine. Mike had a son (who was also a hero) who had a severe case of Cerebral Palsy and who was told he would never walk. Mike worked with that boy every day for hours, even though the work for this loving father was sometimes painful for his son, and even though the odds of him walking were said to be nil because of the severity of his condition. Mike studied everything he could about the disease and lovingly and diligently applied every principle he learned about neural reconditioning to his work with his son. The work was often painful and always exhausting, but he never gave up. That boy, now Mike's grown son and best friend, did indeed learn to walk.

And his father learned to run. After football practices, Mike liked to run us pretty hard (remember this is a 300 pound lineman talking here; hard is a relative term). I was a hard-working veteran player and had a close relationship with Mike, so one day I asked him why, as our coach and leader, he stood on the sidelines and watched us run every day. I told him I felt that he could, and should, run with us, as we were huge guys, and we had already been through a grueling two hour practice. I mentioned the benefits to him, stressing that it would help him stay in shape, and that it would be a great example and highly motivational for the guys. He just looked at me and smiled; he didn't say a word.

The next day, he ran with us, and every single day after that. I promise you this: he got it. He was a real leader — he knew how to lead by example first. And because he got it, he could really teach it. He was a world class coach — he created better people every day through the fine example he set in every part of his life. Everyone on our team loved and respected Mike Bender as a great father, a great human being, and a great leader.

Another friend of mine is a huge believer in the character benefits of sport and wants to do everything he can to raise great athletes. He told me he wanted to get his young hockey playing sons to do some hardcore dry-land training in his backyard, but he was having a hard time motivating them. I explained the whole "leading by example" approach, and that if he wanted his kids to do off-season dry-land training, he should do it with them.

This guy had really let himself go physically over the years, but the truth is this parenting technique works even better when your kids are in better shape than you — they love it, and as a leader you get a chance to display some guts and determination. There is no better way to teach grit, toughness, resolve, commitment, and work ethic than to model it right in front of your kids. Either you model it, or you let it go.

For parents who are considering year round training for their young child, I would like to offer a quick note on dry-land training for young kids, and a short warning about pushing one sport early and hard to give the child a head start with their skills and technique:

Most of the research indicates that this is a very dangerous strategy. Early specialization in one sport (before the age of twelve or so), and specifically, an early introduction to off-season dry-land training is a strong predictor of early burnout, and often results in kids quitting the sport early in their teens. Early specialization is also correlated with higher athlete injury rates. In addition, it denies children the benefits of a wider social network, more interaction with additional adult influences (new coaches) and the long term benefits of being able to compete and have fun in an array of different sports and activities.

If you are determined to get your kids involved in dry-land training make it as fun as possible, and try to incorporate as much "free play" training as possible. Remember, it's the kids who LOVE PRACTICE who eventually succeed in the "marathon of tiny daily improvements" that lead to long term excellence in a particular sport.

If you are serious about learning how to physically prepare your child for sporting excellence, then Google your sport's Long Term Athlete Development Plan, as talented researchers in most developed countries are collaborating to assist young athletes and their coaches in their development. There are also numerous helpful videos online designed to teach specific skills at each level of your child's development.

Model Strong Character as a Teaching Tool

Children become what they see, not what they hear. As a parent, every time the two contradict each other we undermine our own integrity, and over time our own credibility and influence with our child. The very best way to develop our child's character is to step up to the plate and develop our own . . . lead by example.

"Be the change you wish to see in the world."
~ Mahatma Gandhi

Lead By Example:

- *Do what you say you're going to do.*

- *Earn your own respect, and earn your child's respect as a side benefit.*

- *Teach your child character, which is a form of indomitable willpower — a kind of inner strength that keeps you moving forward toward your goals and dreams.*

- *Teach your children, by example, how to keep at things longer than others. You want to show them how you never give up, how you keep plugging forward even when you're tired, and the TV or the Internet is calling, and the results you want seem so far away.*

- *Teach them when you feel like it the least, because those are the moments when you separate yourself from average people and put yourself in a special group — people of strength and character. Live your values. Lead by example.*

> "Never, never, never give up,
> except in matters of honor and good sense."
> ~ Winston Churchill

Absolutely refuse to give up on the small daily steps that will lead you to your dreams. Teach your children about persistence, resolve, self-discipline, mental toughness, and a kind of cheery, indefatigable, unbreakable willfulness that will be more useful to them in the achievement of their goals and dreams than any other quality. Lead by example today, in matters large and small, and give your children a fighting chance to be great.

John D. Rockefeller, once the richest self-made man in the world, wrote the following:

"I do not think there is any other quality so essential to success of any kind as the quality of perseverance. It overcomes almost everything."

Sport taught me this important lesson. I used to be a quitter. Now resolve is one of my two core values. When I first started playing football (at nineteen in university — which was difficult), I had no idea that the game was all about developing character and leadership skills. I thought maybe you were born with or without character, and the last thing I would have described myself as was a leader.

I did not grow up with "sport values", so I thought the game was a recreational activity about something vague that fell under the category of "being a football player" or "being part of a team". Neither of these reasons was deeply motivating. I couldn't see football being an important part of my future, and my thoughts were very often focused on "why" I was even doing what I was doing. I questioned myself over and over, weighing the bad with the good. It certainly used up a lot of my time, energy, and focus. Football wasn't going to help me stay off the farm, and it definitely wasn't easy.

I hung with it because I did like competing; I was making a few good friends, and I had an inspiring, really motivational position coach, although I still didn't really "get it".

It wasn't until I spent some time in the pros under some terrific teachers that I really started to understand that the entire "game within the game" is to become a better version of yourself. I learned about having a "growth mindset" about every aspect of your character and your ability to lead others, not just your skill level. All great coaches demand constant growth and development, and eventually all great players demand this of themselves.

Lessons taught about personal development in sport really can change every aspect of your life.

I learned that the game was all about developing character and leadership skills through hard work and self-discipline. I finally forged that tough, gritty, dig deep kind of resolve and determination, so critical to life success, when I fully understood that the entire experience was about effort and belief. And I finally understood the true meaning of leadership when I figured out the only way to win championships was to develop and serve others so that we could become the best team possible.

Team sport is about setting challenging individual and team goals, and fighting daily for the inch of progress required to achieve those goals. It is about, as heavyweight champion Jack Dempsey once said, "Getting up when you can't".

I believe that even when people are young, they need a strong, compelling "why" to do things, especially when there is hard work involved . . . and I think that kids like the chance to think of themselves in bigger than life, almost heroic ways much more than most of us think. They need to be taught that being a sport success, a sport hero, is about who they are and how they approach the experience, not how much skill or talent they have, or what results they get. I think, as parents and coaches, this "character growth" is what needs to be rewarded, reinforced, explained, and praised as often as possible.

You can't live with courage and conviction unless you have some clarity about who you are and where you're going. You want your children to learn character and leadership from the game they are playing, but you can't ever forget the game is not over for you. You are playing the real thing, every day. It's called life . . . and your character is on the line every time you create a thought or take action.

If you're wondering if you're winning or losing, just look at the results you're getting, and remember that you are 100% responsible for those results.

Integrity in thought and deed is the internal scorecard of the real champion.

- *Figure out what your values are, what you stand for.*

- *Get some clarity about your goals and dreams.*

- *Use this clarity about values and goals to lead by example.*

- *Model your character, for your child, every single day.*

> *"Each morning puts a man on trial and*
> *each evening passes judgment."*
> ~ Roy L Smith

LEARN FROM THE EXPERTS

As an adult, get out of the "lack of self-awareness" fog. Teach your child by your own example. Where you are today is a result of actions you've taken in the past. Your "inner world" is the cause, and your "outer world" is the effect. Learn new things, think new thoughts, take new actions, and get better results. The improvements that you may require to live a balanced, happy, full potential life are far beyond the scope of this short chapter, so if you need help in any of these areas I highly recommend heading to the bookstore to read anything of interest under the self-development heading. Self-improvement books are not for weak, broken people. They're for smart people who want even better results than they're currently getting.

*Check out websites like **www.amazon.com** — there are terrific books on EVERYTHING you need to know to create a much better life, and they are available no matter where you live.*

Learn from the experts, then decide what you're going to do to make your life better, and make that the test, the game, the challenge you face every day. Lead by example. Get in the game.

*If you don't like to read or don't have the time, I recommend the inexpensive life changing self-development audio programs from some of the world's greatest teachers available at **www.nightingaleconant.com.***

Use your commute to work as learning time to become a better parent and a better leader. Or take a few minutes every morning to watch a self-development or leadership video on YouTube. You'll find experts like Brian Tracy, Jim Rohn, John Maxwell, John Gottman, and Carol Dweck. It's free and it's easy. Just do it. Learn all you can.

I believe that leadership starts with the self, and that all leaders are learners. I need quality thoughts, comments, or videos from champions every morning as mental nourishment. Like most parents, I have real issues to face, real challenges . . . and sometimes things have a way of becoming overwhelming. That's life, but having access to the tools and coaching to deal with them makes all the difference.

Keeping my mindset positive, really directing my own focus, my own attitude, and getting some control over the fifty to sixty thousand thoughts I have every day is very important to me. I start each day with a few directed thoughts that inspire gratitude and remind me of my long term goals, and then I read something, listen to something, or watch something educational and inspirational from sources I trust so that I start my day with a winning mindset. I take this little discipline seriously, because I feel that I do myself, my family, and my community a disservice whenever I let this habit slip.

Use your days, each and every one, to build a better life and to lead your child by example. There are no excuses. You can commit to learning everything you need to know; there is no "can" or "can't" when it comes to learning — there is only a "will" or a "won't".

ENJOY MOVING TOWARD YOUR GOALS TODAY AND EVERY DAY

Often parents treat children like they are incomplete, and to some degree they are right.

But so are you, aren't you?

If you're reading this and you are forty years old, aren't you going to be different at forty-five?

Aren't the thoughts, behaviors, habits and actions you choose in the next sixty months, in EACH of the next 1825 days going to affect who you become? Think about it . . .

"He who ceases to be better, ceases to be good."
~ Oliver Cromwell

In the same way you are complete now, your child is complete now. In the same way your child needs to grow and change, you need to grow and change. Life for a child or a parent is NEVER about standing still. Hold yourself to the same "improvement" standard you hold your child to.

"People are not so much *human beings* as they are *"human becomings"*.

I am writing this book as a forty-two year old Dad. I have not seen the inside of a classroom since 1995, and I retired from football five years ago. I have always taken self-improvement seriously, but I believe I have learned more in the last twelve months than I have learned at any prior twelve month period in my life. Each year I expect to learn and grow, and I expect to become a stronger, more skilled version of myself. I have taken this approach for years, and I expect this trend to continue.

Age is not a factor regarding personal growth and development, neither are opportunities to learn in structured schools or athletic environments.

I have my own (constantly growing) list of authors I want to learn from, my own list of life subjects I want to improve in, and my own list of fears I like to chip away at.

I have learned to listen better than I ever listened before. I choose my focus more consistently than I ever have. I have worked on developing better self-discipline, and I have more clarity about my personal values, goals and dreams than ever before.

I created a personal self-improvement program where I continuously change tiny daily habits. I try to take a fluid approach to personal growth — I see myself not as I am, but as **someone I choose to become**. This is obviously not typical of middle-aged men, but it works for me. We are never too old to learn and change. Knowing that you are responsible for shaping the lives of impressionable little ones has a way of forcing you to re-think priorities, words, and actions.

- *Teach your children to enjoy the present by enjoying it yourself.*

- *Teach them how to have fun while moving unerringly in the direction of their long term goals and vision.*

- *Teach them, by your daily example, how to really utilize their days.*

- *You are a mentor and a guide, but never forget you're a teammate as well — learn from your children, and grow and develop like they do!*

So often kids create the negative habit of thinking life will begin when they are sixteen, or nineteen, or twenty-one, and adults look forward to completing university, or when they might get that new job or promotion, or retirement. A friend of mine talked to me the other day about his decision to accept a job he knew he would despise daily for the next 25 years, but after that, he said cheerfully, a pension kicks in and you're "set for life". In the meantime my 38 year old brother, a loving husband and father of two great little boys just got diagnosed with a life threatening brain tumor. Better to live now. There are no guarantees.

Ignoring today while we wait to enjoy an imaginary future can be a sure trap. It is better to set a fine example by living every day to the fullest, and by embracing the fact that, like our children, we are always developing. We need to DIRECT that personal change so that we move unerringly toward our long-term goals while embracing the moment right in front of our faces.

"Forever is composed of nows."
~ Emily Dickinson

We need to enjoy the present like we are five years old again, as if the day is really a "present". Treat it like a gift, and enjoy your time with your loved ones.

Every day is a blank slate, a new gift, and our only objectives should be to use it to enjoy, to love, to laugh, to share, to connect, to serve, and **to improve in the direction of our goals and our highest purpose.** We should lead by example — seize the day, and teach our children by what we do.

Action Steps

1. *AVOID gossip. Gossip is a habit by which you simultaneously destroy your own character and someone else's reputation. If you wouldn't say it to them, don't say it about them.*

2. *Change a small habit every month, or at least one or two meaningful little habits each year (and a hint from someone who does this — make it really, really small — change can be a real battle when you try to do too much too quickly).*

3. *Commit wholeheartedly to the change, put yourself on trial every day, and make it the sport you play.*

4. *Model self-discipline and constant improvement. Don't be fraudulent when you coach character, personal development, goal achievement and self-discipline to your child.*

If appropriate, share with your child the changes you're battling to make to improve your own life. You are both human . . . why not journey together? Why not support, inspire and learn from each other?

Use the space below to record some of the changes you would like to make in your own life:

Chapter Six

"You are worried about seeing him spend his early years doing nothing. What! Is it nothing to be happy? Nothing to skip, play and run around all day long? Never in his life will he be so busy again."

~ Jean-Jacques Rousseau

HAVE FUN (AND ELIMINATE ATHLETIC PERFORMANCE ANXIETY)

What would sport be if it wasn't fun? What would life be? Don't we all die in the end anyway? Living with purpose is the key, but how much better for ourselves and everyone around us when we habitually do it with a cheerful disposition.

Our attitude, the perspective through which we view life, is completely ours to choose, and it can be contagious. The goal for all athletes on a daily basis is to learn as much as they can, work as hard as they can and have as much fun as they can. Hard driving athletes who show up to work every day with a smile on their face are a joy to be around. They attract respect from coaches and peers, and they set a winning tone for any team and eventually any organization.

Experienced athletes know that hard work and fun are not mutually exclusive. In fact, a cheerful disposition makes it possible to work harder and be more energetic than any other mental approach. All great leaders try to have a sense of humor (though none of them are clowns; as a young athlete and future leader it is important to learn that there IS an important difference between the two).

Back in 1996 and 1997 when I played for the Montreal Alouettes, I used to love taking "scout team practice reps" — you'd play against your team's best defensive players and run plays the opposition was going to run when you played them on game day. I had so much fun practicing against our two all star defensive ends. I would draw an imaginary line in the dirt with my foot and make all kinds of outrageous claims about how I was going to dominate the practice period. I didn't care that they were better players. I loved competing. I loved football, and I loved when it got intense.

Naturally the great competitors I faced would rise to the challenge and there would be all kinds of jokes, taunts and comments yelled in from the players not involved in the drill. It became very competitive right away, and enjoyable for all concerned.

We used to laugh and have so much fun competing. I can remember a veteran player, one day coming up to me and saying, "Man, you have no idea how much good you're doing here. Everyone hears you guys competing and laughing, and it just raises the whole level of practice. You make it so easy for the coaches to coach and for the players to compete."

This was like a mini-revelation for me. I was just having fun, competing with my friends, trying to get better; I had no idea that my actions were viewed by team leaders in such a complementary way. Now I really get it, and when I see kids that have fun competing, and help make it fun for the other kids, I feel exactly the way that old veteran player felt on that sunny day back in Montreal.

ENTHUSIASM IS A POWERFUL SPORTS LEADERSHIP ATTRIBUTE

"Enthusiasm is the mother of effort,
and without it nothing great was ever achieved."
~ Ralph Waldo Emerson

Enthusiastic, optimistic, energetic players work harder, recover faster, attract more followers and garner more respect from coaches than players who lack that joyful spark.

Consider the story of Lou Gehrig — he played 2,130 games in a row, and during that time he suffered seventeen fractures with breaks in all eight fingers and both thumbs. When asked why he kept right on playing through all the pain and discomfort of broken bones and fractures, he offered the following insightful statement about the magnificent, hard core, toughening effects of enthusiasm:

"Every time I put on the New York Yankee uniform I get excited!"
~ Lou Gehrig

In general, enthusiasm is the most underrated leadership quality one can have. All great leaders are enthusiastic. There is nothing compelling, charismatic, or attractive about people who grimly work hard with a dour, negative disposition.

One of the critical leadership questions all athletic coaches should ask as they evaluate their potential team captain candidates is, "Who makes it fun to work hard?"

"Very little is needed to make life happy.
It is all within yourself, in your way of thinking."
~ Marcus Aurelius

I've been through some brutal training camps in my football career, and the players that handled that kind of adversity the best were always people with a highly developed ability to laugh and have fun, even though the physical demands and mental pressure were immense.

"Most folks are about as happy
as they make up their minds to be."
~ Abraham Lincoln

These players had been taught a positive approach to athletic success at some point, probably in their very early years. This cheerful, resilient attitude is a choice, and it can be cultivated with practice. Dr John Gray states, "Most adults never really learn how to have fun and enjoy their lives. This is because they didn't get the necessary support to learn how to have fun. Happiness is a skill, and this skill develops between ages seven and fourteen."

The players that had this skill — the ability to have fun while under pressure — didn't do what we called "the math" every night during training camp, working out the depth chart and worrying about whether they were going to be part of the team, or traded or released. They didn't waste their time and mental energy on things they couldn't control. They didn't complain about being sore, or tired, or worried. They were not overly sensitive about constructive feedback from coaches. They worked their tails off, had fun with their teammates, and did their very best every day. They had fun despite the external circumstances.

I learned to think like this when I learned to detach from short-term results. It is amazing how much pride you have when you are young. You fear failure so much, especially if people you like and respect tell you that you are a good player, and they think you are going to be successful. When you are young you are often ill equipped to handle praise, or unexpected adversity, especially when you move to new levels of competition and you are away from your support people.

I ended up in a training camp at the pro level after just two years of university football. I was completely overwhelmed. I had arrived at a level where I was not tactically or mentally ready to compete. I was in way over my head, was thousands of miles from home, and as a result just melted down mentally. It was my lowest experience and point as an athlete. I ended up quitting after just two and a half weeks of training camp, and I felt tremendous shame for months, and to some degree even years, afterward.

I wish someone had taken me aside and given me some advice on how to deal with the fast pace I was on. Every new level attempted as an athlete has the potential to feel like the hardest, most mentally challenging experience of the athlete's life.

The key to succeeding when athletes arrive at these new, uncomfortable levels (levels that are INEVITABLE if your child continues to develop in sport) is to focus on doing your best every day instead of thinking **about the big picture (results)**. It is best to leave that until the experience is over, and just focus on working hard, getting a little better every day, and grabbing a few laughs with your teammates and coaches when you can.

If my kids ever end up in situations like I faced because of my rapid development in sport, I am going to tell them that I will be very proud of them if they do their best every day and that I couldn't care less if they have the talent or skill to make the team. The only thing that matters is that they do their best. I'm also going to tell them to relax and try to enjoy the experience.

Once I adopted this approach my peace of mind as an athlete improved dramatically and my game (and my ability to have fun with my teammates) got a lot better too.

*Don't set your kids up to fail — teach them results don't matter, **approach does**, that they have no control over their God-given talent, nor can they control the competition. The expectation is simply for them to do their best every day in order to be the best they are capable of being.*

John Wooden, arguably the greatest team coach in history, says that the peace of mind associated with that approach is the *only definition of athletic success that matters.*

In my own experience the players that approached training camps or open competitions this way had a huge competitive advantage in terms of their energy levels and the way they were perceived by coaches and teammates. Even if they didn't get the results they wanted, they could leave knowing they had truly done their best. They didn't get caught up in the exhausting negative stress vortex that can be so detrimental to performance under pressure.

EFFECTIVE MENTAL PROGRAMMING FOR YOUNG ATHLETES

Parents can ensure that their children have the same advantage if they arrive at the upper echelons of their sport, where the conditions described above are inevitable. There will be pressure; there will be intense competition, adversity, and fatigue, and all elite athletes deal with injury at some point. These factors are unavoidable and often necessary parts of the ultracompetitive environment. We might as well teach our children to focus only on the things they can control right from the start.

"Weakness of attitude becomes weakness of character."
~ Albert Einstein

As a parent you can prevent an enormous amount of mental anguish in competitive sport or in future challenging life endeavors, if you simply initiate effective mental programming in the first place.

I have conversations all the time about this with my children because I understand how important repetition is as a parent or a coach.

They'll say, "I scored _____ goals today", or, "We won every game but one today" and I'll say, "Great job, but you know I don't care how many goals you score or how many games you win. I care about your effort. On some days you'll score, on some days you won't. On some days you'll win, on some days you'll lose. I care more about how hard you worked, how much fun you had, and what kind of teammate you were. It's those things that make me so proud of you."

Naturally they roll their eyes at dear old Dad, but the message eventually sinks in because I am consistent with it and they hear it often. Then I ask a lot of questions about those same three objectives, or I cite examples of their play or behavior that reinforced this "approach" to this athletic educational experience.

It is important for parents to teach their children from a young age that their daily goals are to work as hard as they can, have as much fun as they can, and to get a little better every day. Effective competitive focus is no different whether a person is 5 or 25. All we have is today, and all we can control is what we think and do right now.

ENTHUSIASM AFFECTS WHO WE ATTRACT AS FRIENDS

Experienced coaches also know enthusiasm is a key leadership quality because it is habitual and it is downloadable. Enthusiastic athletes tend to be enthusiastic most of the time, and their attitude has a dramatic, positive effect on others. Enthusiastic people simply energize the people around them.

Even though it has been twenty years since I played college football, I can still vividly remember the excited feeling I would get every fall because of the incredible enthusiasm and joy that one team captain brought to the experience. His name is Danny Laramee, and he still brings that joy to eighteen to twenty-two year olds as a college football coach. Everyone loves this sparkplug of a guy. He makes it so much fun just to be there, and even more importantly, he makes it so much fun to work hard and compete. In my time, he brought people together, and was a catalyst for making sure guys met each other, that everyone knew what was going on, and that we were all ready to compete and have a great season. I have a lot of great memories because I couldn't help befriending this positive, enthusiastic guy, and the players he coaches today are just as lucky.

My 8 year old daughter Layla tried out recently for an elite under 10 soccer team. Layla is a sweet (often quiet) girl with a "Best Friend Forever" named Jenica. Layla and

Jenica are joined at the hip almost every minute of every day. So when she landed in a group at the elite team tryout without her best friend, and with an array of unfamiliar girls from the surrounding area, I watched with great interest to see what would happen.

Luckily for Layla (and the other girls) there was an enthusiastic leader in her group at that first practice, and Layla had a wonderful sport experience. Immediately after practice, I congratulated my beaming daughter on her hard work and asked her,

"Did you know any of those girls?"

"No", she said.

"Did they know you?"

"One of them knew my name".

"Did you know hers?"

"Not at first", Layla said, "But when she noticed that, she brought everyone together and got each the girls to say their name. After that she said, 'Good job Layla!' every time I did something well, and if I did things wrong she showed me why. Her name is Helen. We're friends now".

Wow, I thought! Enthusiastic leaders are the best. They can transform a challenging experience into something fun and exciting with just a sprinkle of their magic powers. And, as the above example clearly indicates, enthusiastic leaders connect with strangers and turn them into friends with remarkable ease. They are terrific team builders.

Negative people, the polar opposite of enthusiastic people, suck the life out of others, and consequently any team they are associated with. Eventually, positive leaders avoid the exhaustion of spending time with negative teammates. They just drift away, almost like the silent push associated with opposite ends of a magnet. There is a reason why negativity is shunned by great athletes; it is simply too draining on the competitive spirit.

I remember a fun, strong, energetic, positive teammate of mine who played for a different team at the pro level for a number of years, and one off-season he came back to train with me and he was just not his normal chipper self. I asked him what the deal was, why he was being such a downer all the time. I remembered him as a guy who was fun to train with, a guy who loved to compete and who brought a lot of energy and enthusiasm to our off-season workouts. Don't get me wrong, this guy still liked to train hard, but now it was all "resolve" instead of "enthusiasm", and he grimly pushed himself through his training. I asked him what had changed.

He told me he'd shared an apartment for the entire professional football season with a big, tough guy who prided himself on having a very negative attitude. Needless to say, it had been a long, grueling season for my friend because you really are affected by the people you spend the most time with. Once he was out of that environment for a while and back with his old friends, he became his funny, spirited, enthusiastic self again.

> *"You are the average of the five people*
> *you spend the most time with."*
> ~ Jim Rohn

When our children learn to be positive because we teach that valuable skill, we will not only influence how they perform and how they lead, but we influence who their peer group becomes when they are older and more aware of their choices and feelings. Like attracts like, and positive, enthusiastic, success-oriented kids attract the same.

BECOME YOUR CHILD'S POSITIVE INNER VOICE

Kids have a natural enthusiasm, a natural ability to have fun and to believe anything is possible. This wonderful trait gets beaten out of them by overly critical parents who often feel that they are helping them. Children need positive reinforcement to grow up to be enthusiastic leaders. Parents can raise real champions by paying attention to them, then praising their children when they accomplish any of their daily sport goals.

Children need to hear, and then internalize, positive talk so that a powerful inner voice gets created. There is a part of the brain that offers a running commentary on everything we do, and it is usually the voice of one or both of our parents, or that of an early coaching influence.

Dr. Saul Miller, a high performance coach in sport and business, and author of *Performing under Pressure*, states that we think 50,000 to 60,000 thoughts per day. Interestingly, we can only think one thought at a time. We choose those thoughts, and they influence both our feelings and our performance. Most of these thoughts are habitual, and many of them were "programmed" into our minds when we were young. Numerous studies indicate that for most people, between two-thirds and three-quarters of those individual thoughts are negative.

This type of negative self-talk is a recipe for failure in athletics and in life.

Consider the following story from former NHL hockey player Ryan Walter's book, *Off the Bench and Into the Game*:

"After practice I spent a few minutes talking with (legendary hockey leader Mark) Messier about a young Canuck player who had recently joined the club. I suggested to Messier that this player was endowed with considerable talent and stature and should make an impact on the team. Messier agreed with my assessment, but he then confirmed what I suspected. He said, "Yes, I think you're right Ryan, but *he will have to greatly improve his self-talk to reach his potential.*"

Self-talk is an important part of the athletic development process, and it is an area where parents play a crucial role.

Don't be the one responsible for turning your child into a negative, critical pessimist whose strongest personality traits are useless worry, anxiety and stress. Teach them to be strong, positive, enthusiastic, action oriented doers and leaders. Teach them positive self-talk so they never lose that natural enthusiasm, that energetic spark that is so necessary as they drive toward their goals.

*Kids have to learn that sport is simply about doing your best, trying to improve every day, and having fun. They have to learn to focus on this powerful approach prior to, and while they're competing. If you, as a parent, take this approach and **reinforce*** *it consistently, day in and day out, like a family mantra, then your children will revert to this approach when pressure situations occur. They will stay focused on their approach, on what they have to do to succeed. This is how winners perform under pressure. It takes mental discipline from years and years of positive reinforcement, and it starts with you, the influential parent.*

I remember listening to Dean Smith in an interview talking about his most famous college athlete, Michael Jordan, and how he approached practice. He said he'd never seen anyone compete in practice like Jordan did from the very first day he showed up at North Carolina until the day he left to become an NBA legend. Apparently, initially, he was not the best player North Carolina had, but he outworked everyone every day. He pushed himself to win every drill. Dean Smith said even as a relatively unskilled rookie, Jordan forced his team to victory in scrimmages after practice on a daily basis. Coach Smith said it happened daily regardless of who his teammates were — if team A won, Coach Smith would put Michael on team B and then they would win. Jordan was an approach-driven player, and his approach was to compete at his very highest level every minute of every practice.

In competitive team sports that approach, that daily competitive drive and willingness to work makes you an instant leader. Jordan's adherence to this approach on a daily basis for years made him one of the toughest competitors in the history of basketball. His approach led directly to the results he got later in his playing career. He is widely recognized by many as the greatest basketball player in history. He also co-authored a great little 36 page book suitable for kids that impacted my athletic career profoundly as a 28 year old. It is called *I Can't Accept Not Trying*.

All champions know that pressure is an illusion; fear is an illusion. There is only the athlete's approach to the moment, and that approach should always be the same. The approach becomes one of full effort at all times, with enthusiasm and positive expectation — really seeing the opportunities for success, not failure, so the athlete is aggressive and proactive.

PUT YOURSELF IN YOUR CHILD'S REALITY

Sport is not fun when you are in a pressure situation focused on results. You get paralyzed by thoughts of personal failure and embarrassment compounded by disappointing your loved ones. That's a nightmare mental state and it leads to negative results as well, which then perpetuate fear and performance anxiety.

> *"Life is like playing a violin solo in public,*
> *and learning the instrument as one goes along."*
> ~ Samuel Butler

Sport is a public challenge, a public learning experience. It is important to not sit on the sidelines for even a minute and make the mistake of forgetting what it is like to perform in public while still learning. It can be very daunting for a child to be challenged continuously. Parents must provide constant support and enthusiasm.

- *So please, please, enough with the criticism of ANY child out there, let alone your own special little person.*

- *Laugh and enjoy the growth and development of all the kids in the competition.*

- *Focus on creating a winner through positive reinforcement.*

- *Create a happy winner — encourage your child to have fun.*

"The most deadly of all sins is the mutilation of a child's spirit."
~ Erik Erikson

It is our responsibility as parents to frame our children's mental state when they are young so that they have a strong mental approach to pressure situations when they are older. They must learn to face challenging situations with a relaxed "approach driven" mental state that results in peak performance (and peak enjoyment).

"Success is a state of mind. If you want success,
start thinking of yourself as a success."
~ Joyce Brothers

Preparing our children for sport (and life) challenges is not rocket science. It is simply being diligent, day in and day out, about what we reinforce. Sport, and life, are about our attitude (how we view it) and our approach (what we do to prepare, to hone our skills and talents so that when the situation arrives, we are ready and confident).

We are the key to our child's long term development in sport — we must use the power of repetition, even when our child shrugs it off and seems to ignore us. We are a major positive influence in our child's life, and they do listen even when they act like they don't.

Our positive talk will become their positive self-talk, and we will create a positive, enthusiastic athlete who loves the entire learning experience. We must comment on their hard work, comment on some tiny improvement we notice (because we are actually paying attention to our child's development), tell them they look great out there, they look like a great teammate and a winner.

You can prepare your child to relax and enjoy life challenges by reinforcing the right mental approach at an early age in sport. You can create a "success pattern" deep in the child's subconscious mind that the child will refer back to during the inevitable future challenges that leaders and successful people face on their journey to the top.

Action Steps

1. *Re-evaluate how you view sport.*

2. *See it as "experiential character training".*

3. *Take it seriously — be there and be observant.*

4. *Be supportive and have fun.*

5. *Praise progress so that your child learns positive self-talk, creates a healthy self-concept, and retains that natural child-like enthusiasm all kids are born with.*

List some of the attributes your child displays that you are proud of and want to reinforce:

Chapter Seven

*"The prime purpose of being four is to enjoy being four —
of secondary importance is to prepare for being five."*
~ Jim Trelease

SPEND TIME TOGETHER

*"The deepest principle in human nature
is the craving to be appreciated."*
~ William James

Have you read the popular, profound little book by Mac Anderson and Lance Wubbels entitled, *To a Child Love is Spelled T-I-M-E?* It is a very simple book, probably a 5 or 10 minute read, but a definite thought-provoker for busy parents. The concept is simple — nothing is more valuable to a child than a parent's undivided, loving attention.

Constant excuses and procrastination teach children that they are not important, or at least not as important as routine errands, meaningless phone conversations, or the addictive pull of the television, I-phone, Blackberry or other personal entertainment or communication devices.

The allocation of our time teaches our children what our priorities are, and consequently, what our values are. Children with high self-esteem share their parents' strong character and positive values because they have been consistently exposed to those values. The parents have lived them via their everyday choices. On a day to day basis, wise parents discipline themselves to do what really matters — and the simple truth is, to our children, nothing matters more than our precious time.

> *"Lost, yesterday, sometime between sunrise and sunset,*
> *two golden hours each set with sixty diamond minutes.*
> *No reward is offered for they are gone forever."*
> ~ Horace Mann

Studies indicate that most people waste a staggering 35 to 50 hours a week watching television or surfing the net recreationally or on social media. Too many parents are unconsciously addicted to these plug-in drugs, and it has affected their ability to spend time with their children. I know this isn't you, and if you asked every parent in your neighborhood, they could pass a lie detector test saying that it is not them either. Nevertheless, the statistics don't lie.

Are you aware of the time you spend watching television, using computers, surfing the Internet, or on Facebook? Could this be eroding the quality of the most important relationships in your life? Is this creating the illusion of "busyness" or "overwhelm" in your life?

SPORT CAN BE VALUABLE TIME TOGETHER

Sport can successfully be marketed to children as "time together". There is nothing more valuable to children in their early years than "special time" with parents. Parents sometimes tell themselves stories about their children not caring about this, but they are usually just that — stories told to justify not putting the time in doing what should be their most important work.

By being present, being attentive, having fun with our children, and taking the time to teach the lessons from sport in a transferrable way that affects the child's perspective on other areas of his or her life, we really can create "special time" around sport where all our values are taught in a fun and highly successful manner.

"Your children need your presence more than your presents."
~ Jesse Jackson

Consider the following example about a family who successfully raised three highly successful children with terrific values and character. In November 2010 *Success* magazine did a cover story on the Manning family — a family of five, with three Hall of Fame caliber, NFL football players. Archie, the father, made the following three points:

1. "I just loved being with my kids, that's all. I made (my kids) part of my life as well as insinuating myself into theirs."

2. "I'm a firm believer that the first two tenants of effective child-rearing boil down to "spend a lot of time with your children' and 'cherish them,'" Archie writes, "because, one, they need you when they're growing, and two, they're going to be up and gone before you realize it."

3. "Once you have kids, your responsibility is to the whole family." The Mannings committed to having at least one parent represented at each of the (3) boys events . . . one week, Archie logged a total of 17 basketball games."

From the day your child is born you, as a parent, dictate what kind of relationship you'll have with your child. Your child will reciprocate, or "mirror" your example as the years pass. There should be nothing more important to you than the opportunity to raise a positive, goal-directed, happy, well-adjusted, child with strong character and ingrained leadership skills. Sport can be a huge ally in this endeavor which should be why you invest your time and money in organized sport for your child.

To the child, however, the long-term character building benefits of sport have no attraction. Some kids gravitate to sport because it's fun, but very often, to get your child to "buy in" to sport, you have to "sell" the benefits of sport to your child as "time together" because that's what they care about when they are very young.

Then you have to make it so — you have to arrange your life so you can participate in this important leadership training and character development activity. And you have to have fun with it.

This requires an investment on your part — you have to allocate the time and focus required to be there on time, to be relaxed and attentive to the child's development, and you want to make it fun for the child so that they continue to want to participate in and receive the full benefits of organized sport.

MAKE TEACHING LIFE VALUES THROUGH SPORT A TOP PRIORITY

Very often parents treat sport as a low priority item that is a seen as a sacrifice they are making for their children. Not so. This is a terrible parental strategy toward one of the most important developmental influences in a child's life. In our western culture we will never have a better opportunity to positively affect our children's character and leadership development than by reinforcing the potential life lessons available through organized sport.

When I went to Acadia University I competed on the football team and completed a degree in Political Science with Honors; later I completed a Master's degree. I learned a great deal from my studies, made some terrific friends, and developed skills like self-discipline and attention to detail. Nevertheless, it was my participation in Acadia University Football — the hands-on, get knocked down, get dirty, get hurt, lose games, compete to get on the game day roster, compete to earn a starting position, compete to win games part of the university experience that taught me the most.

I learned the most about overcoming adversity and dealing with difficult people. I met the greatest friends I will ever have. I learned about trying to achieve a common goal together (and you don't have to be an adult very long before you learn how important THAT skill is — life truly is a team game). I received some very influential mentoring from members of the university coaching staff, particularly from our head coach, Sonny Wolfe. I also learned at least as much about self-discipline and attention to detail as I did in the academic part of school.

Sport, coached effectively (and reinforced repeatedly by you, the most important influence in your child's life) really is EXPERIENTIAL CHARACTER DEVELOPMENT AND LEADERSHIP TRAINING. It is important work, and it is not work you want to underperform at during the formative years when your influence is most powerful.

"Sport ideally teaches discipline and commitment.
It challenges you and builds character for everything you do in life."
~ Howie Long

You do not want to raise a problematic adult who knows nothing about the character attributes and daily discipline required to achieve long-term success. Involve your children in organized sport and teach them the good stuff — the life skills and attitude that will free them to succeed in any endeavor. Chances are, if your child fails to become a responsible adult, you will regret this missed developmental opportunity for decades to follow.

Action Steps

1. *Take personal responsibility for how you live your life, and how you behave on a day to day basis. Someone once said, "Show me your schedule and I'll show you your values."*

2. *Cut out some of the useless stress-inducing garbage in your life like overuse of screen time.*

3. *Create some space in your life. Then do more of the stuff that really matters, like paying attention to your child's positive development, and reinforcing it every chance you get.*

4. *Children naturally love to laugh, play, do activities and generally have fun. Set a goal to have at least a few minutes of fun with each child every day.*

5. *Let the days add up to a lifetime of small, happy memories. Spell your love T-I-M-E to your child on a daily basis. Walk the walk.*

Record your daily activities for the next few days and become more aware of what you value.

Chapter Eight

While we try to teach our children all about life,
Our children teach us what life is all about.
~ Angela Schwindt

ALLOW YOUR CHILDREN TO INFLUENCE YOU

One of the most powerful coaching tools you can use with your children is to let THEIR transferrable skill development affect YOUR life skill development. Reinforce their lessons by allowing them to teach you.

"Children reinvent your world for you."
~ Susan Sarandon

Simply make statements like, "You know what? You worked so hard at practice today that I'm going to try to do the same tomorrow and see if I can get more done in less time."

This is very powerful stuff. It allows your children to feel like an equal from a self-esteem standpoint. Saying to your child,

"I see you doing all this exercise . . . I want to be just like you so I'm going to start _____ tomorrow, and see if I can stick to it like you do." This reinforces their character development by letting them lead you.

This technique is particularly important for demanding parents who struggle to lead by example. These parents are often unnecessarily critical because they have forgotten (or never learned) how difficult even the smallest personal improvements can be.

The technique is to teach your child by waking up and getting into the personal development game yourself. Adult life only differs from that of a child's because the activities are different — you still need to learn, and then do, and you need to find ways to improve. You still need to take risks, learn new skills, and embrace new challenges. Even as adults we never stop learning.

> **"The man who views the world the same way at 50 as he did at 20 has wasted 30 years of his life."**
> ~ Mohammed Ali

Let your children teach you to learn and grow. This is one of the most effective self-esteem builders you can use with your children. It forces you to lead by example; it creates a deeper bond with your children; it accelerates the maturity process as they begin to see you as a fellow human being instead of only perceiving you in a parenting role, and it provides extra motivation and support for you to follow through on meaningful changes and improvements you would like to make.

Three important tools for personal goal achievement are:

1. Set clear goals

2. Tell supportive people

3. Track your progress

When you involve your child in your own self-development process you activate all three of these helpful tools. The process of articulating to a child what you're trying to accomplish necessitates clarity. Children can provide wonderful support because they love you unconditionally, and children have a way of holding you accountable. In fact, most parents can vouch for their child's amazing ability to notice every one of their parental inconsistencies. Use your children's support to help you become a better person. Involve them in your life as you attempt to stay engaged in theirs.

COMMUNICATE DAILY AND SHARE EXPERIENCES

This personal development connection can be further accelerated when you start to share experiences with your children through daily dialogue. Become a learner with your child. Ask them questions every day, and share personal struggles and lessons you are experiencing on your journey. Questions like the following are very powerful conversation starters:

1. What was the most fun thing that happened to you today?

2. What's your favorite part of practice (or school)?

3. How did you feel when you and Susie weren't getting along?

4. What should we do for fun this Sunday?

5. Where should we go on vacation this year?

Children who grow up in a non-dictatorial family, where they feel they have some input, grow up to be more confident and thus better leaders. They learn from a very early age to think for themselves, and this external recognition of their spoken opinion validates their self-worth. They learn to find their voice, and that their opinion matters. They are part of a democracy — the true family unit. Children learn to influence, which, along with a compelling vision, are the two most important attributes shared by all great leaders. Children in democratic families also learn the most lucrative business and sales skill on the planet — the art of negotiation. The parent is the experienced guide and mentor, and always makes the final call. The truly enlightened parent also understands, however, that the parental role involves tremendous sharing, loving, and learning with, and through, the child.

LEARN FROM EACH OTHER

*"Every child is an artist. The problem is
how to remain an artist once he grows up."*
~ Pablo Picasso

The approach that "I am here to learn from my children" as well as to guide them is a healthy mindset that takes enormous pressure off the parent to be "right all the time" or to "have all the answers".

Communication with children can be used to influence behavior in both directions. Children need to be guided, and there are times when a parent's experience, wisdom and discipline are necessary.

There are other times, however, when parents should ask themselves the following questions:

1. Who is more creative, my child or me?

2. Who is better at living in "the now", the only reality that truly exists?

3. Who is better at having fun?

4. Who takes more risks, and thus consistently reaps surprising rewards, my child or me?

5. Who is better at asking for things they want?

6. Who is more open-minded?

7. Who is more open to learning new things?

8. Who is more comfortable asking for help when they need it?

9. Who has fewer prejudices?

10. Who has mastered simplicity?

11. Who exercises more?

Often, despite my efforts to be positive and optimistic, I become just another stressed-out, full speed, overwhelmed middle-aged man. I rely on my kids to remind me of what it is really all about. They are so great at having fun, at loving, at staying in the moment. They are the world's greatest huggers, and sometimes, at the end of a long hard day, I really need them for that.

We are a team, and their job is to keep it real — my problems are always temporary, worrying never helps, and I never "fix" anything significant in the evening anyway, which seems to be my time of highest stress. They remind me that I need to laugh, indulge in some fun, stay connected with the lighter side of life, and stay young at heart. I force myself to switch gears, because truthfully, little people are great at teaching big people about what's truly important. I don't want to bring them into my world of adult issues — I want to join their world of love and fun.

Relax and enjoy being a parent. You have a very important role to play as an influential guide and experienced mentor in your child's life. But you also have a role to play as a companion, a fellow traveler, privileged to share a loving bond with your child. Enjoy the experience of sharing your different perspectives, and remain open to being influenced by your child.

Action Steps

1. *Lose the control thing. Create a more democratic environment.*

2. *Learn to lead by asking questions and really listen to input from the most important people in your life.*

3. *Make sure you're really "present" at the dinner table.*

4. *Start to ask questions about things that involve the whole family.*

5. *Ask your child to inspire your self-discipline and development. Allow them to influence you. Teach them that they can be important leaders in your world.*

List several things you could learn from your child then communicate with him or her about what you're learning through their example.

_____

_____

_____

_____

_____

_____

Chapter Nine

*Anyone who thinks the art of conversation is dead
ought to tell a child to go to bed.*

~ Robert Gallagher

DAILY IMPROVEMENT

The entire focus for parents following practices should be directed toward reinforcing the skills of listening to coaches, working hard, having fun, and improving slightly every day. Most psychology literature indicates that self-worth comes from encouragement and praise, and a parent's goal is to raise a child with a strong sense of self-worth.

It is healthy for children to like praise but not to need it, which is exactly how they will feel if they are used to receiving it from you during their developmental years.

*Pay attention to what your child does at practice or during games, and reinforce the **approach** you're teaching by using well directed praise.*

COACHING AND PARENTING A HIGH SELF-ESTEEM CHILD

Failure and discouragement are a big part of succeeding in life, and you want your child's self worth to be so ingrained that they make the necessary adjustments to failure and adversity without losing hope.

Self-esteem developed when a child is young becomes a mental buffer against criticism and adversity later in life. It is a parent's job to build a child's self-worth in preparation for the challenges which he or she will inevitably face on the journey to success.

> *"To establish true self-esteem we must concentrate on our successes and forget about the failures and the negatives in our lives."*
> ~ Dr Dennis Waitley

Constant criticism while a child is developing destroys self-worth and creates weak children who are fearful and who give up easily. Often well-meaning parents criticize their children in sport "for their own good" not realizing that their job is to strengthen their children's character.

My personal belief is that criticism is damaging most of the time whether we are coaching a child or an adult. No one responds well to criticism. It can be used effectively on a team or in a group, where it doesn't feel like a personal attack, and you have the support of teammates to buffer the sting a little, but generally, criticism should be but a tiny part of a good coach or parent's repertoire.

Great coaches are teachers first. They explain, and demonstrate, and walk you through things, and allow you to experiment and make mistakes; then they teach some more, and redirect, and allow you to experiment again, and make some more mistakes; then they redirect again.

One of the best young coaches I experienced in the CFL was a guy named Rick Campbell who would begin every coaching opportunity with this line, or one very similar: "I really appreciate your effort here, but you can get this done a lot easier if you . . ."

I would sit there and smile as he effortlessly redirected proud, professional athletes (who had made mistakes, some of which lost games for us) in front of as many as fifty or sixty of their peers.

His coaching never felt like a personal attack because he respected the player's effort (which was often a reflection of their character).

He would then correct their technique (which was something they felt empowered to improve).

He always coached like he was on their side, like he had little tips and secrets that would help them succeed more effectively in the future.

He never coached like he was assigning blame.

There are so many similarities between kids and professionals. Most parents and early educators know about using the "three strikes" principle to discipline children.

This technique is designed to give children time to assess what they are doing, to consider the penalty for continuing their current behavior, and perhaps pay the price (usually a time-out) if they continue.

I watched an old, tough coach I had at the pro level use this very technique on a player who felt being, "just on time," or a "minute or two late" for meetings was acceptable.

The talented rookie walked into the meeting a minute late and Coach Mac said, "Hey Joe, you ever play baseball?"

"Yeah."

"You know how you get three strikes and you're out?"

"Yeah."

"Well this is strike one. You understand what I'm saying?"

"Yeah coach, I got it."

A couple of weeks later the same thing happened.

"Joe, you remember what I was saying about baseball and three strikes and you're out?"

"Yeah."

"Well that's strike two."

A month or so later we were on the road for a game in Hamilton and we had an afternoon meeting in our hotel. Joe showed up late, claiming his alarm clock had failed him.

Mac didn't seem too concerned.

We played the game, flew home, and the next day we had our usual run down and meetings. Everyone was seated, ready to start the film session.

Mac is at the front of the room with the video remote in his hand, ready to start the meeting, when he says,

"Hey Joe, remember what I told you about baseball and three strikes?"

"Yeah."

"Well yesterday was strike three and you're out."

"What do you mean coach?"

"I mean get out of here. Go clean out your locker; you're done."

The incredulous rookie running back, our first round draft pick that year, left the room with a life-lesson in hand. The question is, did the Edmonton Eskimos cut him, or did he cut himself? Were his parents partly responsible for not teaching him about the price of consistent tardiness?

Maybe his Mom and Dad didn't use three strikes, or maybe they never followed through on the punishment part of it, or maybe they were the kind of parents who drove him to practice a few minutes late every day, developing a pattern he would continue for years. . . Who knows?

A complementary relationship exists, even at the pro level, between "parenting work" and "coaching work". For coaching to be really effective, parents have to do their work well. Well parented kids are a coach's dream.

If the parent does the basic work of teaching manners, punctuality, and respect, and keeps a close eye on the child's approach, the coach can do his or her basic work more easily. Together parents and coaches can use the challenges involved in sport to teach character and leadership.

Sport itself, because it is so competitive and challenging by definition, will provide the child a myriad of critical growth opportunities. Coaches teach players skills, design and run effective practices, and balance player development with winning, depending on the specific goals of the program. The parent's job is to nurture and support the child's character development, and to reinforce the transferrable skills the child is developing through this valuable training experience.

BUILDING YOUR CHILD'S CONFIDENCE

"If you hear a voice within you say 'You cannot paint' then by all means paint, and that voice will be silenced."
~ Vincent Van Gogh

Self-worth and self-esteem are constants that do not vary despite challenges like learning new skills or trying new activities. Self-esteem can be defined as how we feel about ourselves in general. Self-esteem can improve significantly through our own efforts, though at an early age much of our "reputation with ourselves" is determined by how our loved ones perceive and treat us. Parents play an enormous role in the development of a child's self-esteem. Hence the earlier comments on unconditional love, and developing the feeling in our children that "they are enough as they are".

Developing confidence is different from developing self-esteem; confidence comes from practice. It comes from hard work and repetition. Cancer survivor and champion cyclist Lance Armstrong put it this way, "The world is full of people who are trying to purchase self-confidence, or manufacture it, or simply posture it. But you can't fake self-confidence, you have to earn it, and if you ask me, the only way to do that is work."

As parents we must understand that practice is more than skill development — it is character development. Working hard at practice day in and day out can forge self-confidence and strong character. Understanding the value of putting the work in on something you care to become excellent at is a LEARNED approach. And when our children understand this one concept, they will be half way to achieving excellence in any area they choose from that point onward. Confidence is an authentic, real feeling that derives from knowing we put the work in, that we did our very best, in the time we had available, to get ready.

"Confidence is preparation.
Everything else is beyond your control."
~ Richard Kline

Confidence is NOT a constant, and can easily vary from sport to sport. For example, someone who is a very confident skier can be a very fearful swimmer. Confidence can be skill specific, or sport specific, or activity specific.

Building confidence comes from repeatedly exposing ourselves to a new challenge or growth opportunity, and letting repetition ease our inner discomfort. Confidence continues to grow as practice leads to mastery.

> *"If people knew how hard I worked to gain my mastery, it wouldn't seem so wonderful."*
> ~ Michelangelo

Parents need to understand the value of practice as a confidence builder, and they must live this value by respecting the "practice" process as much as the "game" process. Games are about performance and results, both of which stem from the practice process. Much like real life, the commitment to background work leads to great results. Authentic, well-earned confidence is derived from putting the work in daily.

My sport/school experiences began to define me in my early twenties. My hard work and dedication started paying off, and I was beginning to like and trust myself. I developed a reputation with myself about following through on my commitments to run stairs, work my technique, lift weights, play basketball and squash, study at least an hour for every hour of class time, and never miss class. I was doing what I told myself I would do, so naturally my self-esteem was reaping the rewards of that approach.

I was becoming a more confident student, and I grew from someone who was nervous about speaking in class to someone who wrote term papers because I could not come to an agreement with professors on hotly debated classroom topics. I was also becoming a more confident athlete.

I can still remember being surprised (and deeply pleased) when my classy head coach described me to my parents as one of the hardest workers on the team. I know they were quite surprised, as I had been a terribly disinterested, bored farm worker for most of my youth.

My life had changed, and become much more enjoyable and rewarding, because I had finally learned how to take small daily steps toward long-term, personally relevant goals. Now I want to teach these skills to my children, and help other parents teach their children, so kids clearly understand this approach at eight or ten instead of at twenty or thirty.

There are no shortcuts; the elevator to the top is always broken, and people really do achieve mastery and ultimately success one step at a time. We have to EARN success in sport and life. It is great to have big dreams, big goals, and big wants, as long as we understand that life (or our competition) doesn't care what we want, or even what we need. Life and sport only give us what we deserve, and what we deserve stems directly from what we earn through repetitive, intelligently directed work and sacrifice.

BUILDING YOUR CHILD'S MENTAL TOUGHNESS AND RESOLVE

"The harder you work the harder it is to surrender."
~ Vince Lombardi

Daily work and a commitment to constant improvement lead to great resolve. Donald Trump, a tough businessman who had very supportive parents who taught him to push forward through adversity, described his business experiences this way, "I was relentless, even in the face of total lack of encouragement, because much more often than you'd think, sheer persistence is the difference between success and failure."

Resolve, or the unwillingness to give up in the face of adversity, may be the most important quality for success in any life endeavor. We must take every opportunity to teach our children, through sport, that daily hard work toward our goals regardless of our immediate results is the secret to developing tremendous resolve and great mental toughness.

Daily work is the key to forging strong character, which is the foundational piece to becoming a great athlete, a great person, a great leader, a great contributor, a great success. We must support our child through well directed, honest praise. We must teach them to work hard and be relentless, so that when that support is not there later on, when those big, lonely, scary, life and business challenges come along, they will have internalized our supportive voice and created a belief in their own ability to persevere through hard, determined, daily effort.

All people are 96 to 98% habitual. All successful people have successful habits. Most habits take at least a month to become semiautomatic. After another month or two they become more and more ingrained, requiring less and less attention and focus. Eventually our habits become part of us, and part of our identities.

Action Steps

1. *Create a tiny, easy-to-implement habit that will have a big effect on your life or your family.*

2. *Stick with it.*

3. *Teach your children about hard work, daily improvement, and gritty, mental toughness (resolve) through YOUR EXAMPLE FIRST.*

4. *Then draw positive comparisons to their efforts in sport.*

Chapter Ten

We've had bad luck with our kids — they've all grown up.
~ Christopher Morley

CHERISH THE HONOR YOU'VE BEEN GRANTED

Ever listen to parents who have conditioned themselves to believe that parenting is the most difficult job they will ever have — parents who complain, and complain, and complain, and then wonder why they fail to raise positive successful children?

Parenting is an honor, and our results will mirror our attitude toward that immense responsibility. We have the best job in the world. Done well, nothing influences the state of the world more than highly skilled, positive parenting.

> *"There is no friendship, no love,*
> *like that of the parent for the child."*
> ~ Henry Ward Beecher

By choosing to achieve a level of conscious competence about what we are trying to achieve as a parent, and then using the masterful (and free) tools available to us — unconditional love, positive support, daily communication and sincere role modeling, nothing we ever do will transcend the experience we have raising our children. It is a total win-win . . . wonderful, successful kids, and the life-altering, positive transformational process all great teachers go through.

SET CLEAR PARENTING GOALS

It all starts with having clear goals. What if we raise children who really know we will love them forever, no matter what? Imagine how they will feel about us as we age and they mature into powerful, responsible adults?

Imagine raising children who look challenges straight in the eye and never step back, paralyzed by fear and inadequacy?

Imagine raising children who believe life is about helping other people, about sharing their talents and skills to ease some of the pain and hurt in the world?

What if we raise someone who becomes a great leader, someone who really makes a positive difference in the world? How would that make us feel? What would that process, including the changes we need to make to lead by example, have on us, and on what we become over the years?

Jobs come and go. Even friends come and go. The house can be cleaned and fixed later. The TV and the computer will still be there long after the kids are out the door. But we will be parents until we die or our children die. Parenting is the most rewarding job we will ever have, and done well, it is the most rewarding. We as parents have created a child — what a wondrous miracle! We must now get to work and do our job as a parent. No excuses.

If you think this book is written by a guy who has all the time in the world to spend with his kids, you are wrong, but I make time. I've mismanaged my life to the extent that I start work around 5:00 a.m. and end work around 5:30 p.m.

I've made football mistakes, investment mistakes, and business mistakes. Basically I'm saying I'm no better at life than anyone else. I do, however, have a very specific goal that overrides every other demand in my life. I want to be a great family man. I want to be a great husband, and more than anything else, I want to be a great father. I make sure I get my family time in no matter how "busy" I am. It's that important.

I have breakfast at home with my loved ones; I get on the floor and play, all two hundred and eighty pounds of me. I give and get lots of hugs and they keep me going. Nothing rivals the warmth and security of small hands clinging and squeezing in a giant embrace.

I take my kids camping. We laugh. We love. I give them all the love and energy that I can. I hug my beautiful wife in front of the children, and I tell her that I love her all the time. Children need to see love between their parents no matter what their circumstance. I attend every practice and game possible despite being "busy". My life is crazy; it's messy; it's often difficult, it's always interesting, and I appreciate every bit of it because I focus on what really matters most of the time — my family.

"There are only two ways to live your life.
One is as if nothing is a miracle.
The other is as though everything is a miracle."
~ Albert Einstein

We should never, never, never prioritize the urgent over the important in our lives. We can't let the media, teachers, coaches, the Internet, or our children's peer groups be the most important influences in our children's lives. We must truly appreciate the importance of our work as parents. We need to think through our responses, our actions, and the examples we are setting.

OUR VALUES

We need to step up, create some family values, and live them every day. Values are not something we write down and forget about. They are something to live by, affecting the daily choices we make and the actions we take. Our values should never change, and when we lay on our deathbed all our loved ones should be able to gather around us and talk about our values even if we never articulated them to anyone simply because we spent years living them day in and day out.

"The best inheritance a parent can give his children is a few minutes of his time each day."
~ Orlando A. Battista

The first family value we should establish is that we value our family. How? We put our time in. We put our attention, and our focus, on our children. Love and laugh with them every day. Really listen. Look them right in the eye and tell them how much you love them and how proud you are of them. Rise to the challenge to be the most important influence in our child's life, and change their world forever.

The second value we establish should be our integrity. How? We follow through on our commitment to be the best parents we can possibly be. We walk the walk. We live our values starting right now. We work to raise positive, happy children who will bless the world long after we are gone.

Action Steps

The next time you walk by that messy bedroom, or look in frustration at the toys on the living room floor, or you complain about the noise and the commotion and the constant interruptions and requests, just think ahead ten or twenty years to when you're going to look into that same bedroom and those toys are going to be gone, and the house is going to be too quiet, and you're going to wonder where the time went and you're going to miss it all so, so much. Enjoy the little helmets and the little gloves and the little shoes and the "big" games and the friends and the scraped knees and the 7 a.m. practices . . . because when they're gone, they're gone forever.

1. Stop and think that you only have your children with you for a short time, and what a miracle it is that they are there at all; try to appreciate being a parent, and appreciate the fact that your child or children are with you for the moment, and all you have to do is be with them too.

2. Thank your children after they're tucked in at night for the great honor of being their Mom/Dad. Tell them it's the most important job in the world because they are so very special and that you're going to do the very best you can.

3. Thank God, nature, the Universe, Fate, something or someone bigger than yourself every day for the privilege (gift) of getting to nurture your very own special child.

4. Love them by having fun with them every day, and live each day like your children are only with you for a little while.

Intention precedes attention. In other words, how you look at someone influences what you see. Why not use the space remaining to list all the things you love about your family members? Then when you really look at the people you love, you'll see the wonderful qualities you listed here. You'll also enjoy looking back on this list when your little one is a big one like you!

_____

_____

_____

_____

_____

_____

_____

_____

_____

_____

Please visit *www.littleathletesbigleaders.ca* today to sign up for our daily sport excellence message. Many parents share these inspiring, informative messages with their little athletes daily. These wonderful sport parents want to maximize their influence during the youth sport years as they work to raise confident, happy leader who will do great things in the world.

Appendix 1

"Leaders are not born. They are made.
They are made just like anything else . . . through hard work.
That's the price we have to pay to receive that goal or any goal."

~ Vince Lombardi

LEADERSHIP RESOURCES FOR COACHES, PARENTS, AND MATURE PLAYERS

I don't believe children should be "team captains" on a season long basis until at least the age of 11 or 12. Their level of awareness is too limited, and even more importantly, the children that are "passed over" in this process are denied the important (and very true) belief that they can become a great leader like some of their sport heroes.

Once children are old enough to learn what leadership is, and what the responsibilities of a team leader are, and they can assess where they stand in relation to others attempting to learn and use those important skills, then and only then should coaches begin to reward players with the title and responsibilities of "team leadership".

Fortunately, however, some of the foundational principles of leadership can be taught at a very young age. For example, the wise and committed coaches of my son's team (6 and 7 year olds) bought two hard-hats and stuck a team logo on the front of each. They then pick the two hardest workers from each game, and they win the coveted "hardest worker of the game" award. I suspect, in time, that each of the little rascals on the team will feel the tremendous pride that comes from being acknowledged by their coaches for this important leadership trait.

Ready to become a team leader in organized team sport?

The following is a list of principles created by myself and my long time friend and teammate Dan Comiskey after we had a collective 25 years experience in professional football and four Grey Cup championships, but prior to Dan coming out of retirement as a leadership trainer to lead the Calgary Stampeders in 2010 as a mature player. Dan was brought in to play, but also to lead, by an excellent professional coach name John Hufnagel.

"Huff" had coached the likes of football greats Peyton Manning, Tom Brady and Doug Flutie, and Dan's goal was to put himself in that esteemed group as a team leader in Huff's estimation. In order to do that, we had to spend a couple of days tapping into our experiences as players, leadership trainers, and authors. We wanted to create some clarity around Dan's attempt to be the best team leader possible that season, and after a couple of days of effort, thought and reflection we feel we have done so.

While all of the leadership principles are important, the most important principle is at the peak of the pyramid, and they become less so toward the base.

They should be taught in that sequence as well.

For example, when my six year old asked me on the way home from hockey practice one day, "Dad, how do you become a captain?" My response was simple, "That's easy Sam," I said. "You just make sure you're the hardest worker at practice every single day."

If Sam had been ten, or sixteen, or even twenty-six, we would have had a much more detailed discussion about the different elements of team leadership outlined in the leadership pyramid.

PRINCIPLES OF TEAM LEADERSHIP

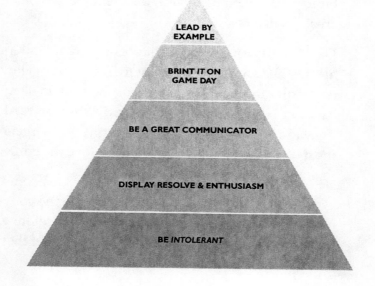

LEAD BY EXAMPLE

BRINT IT ON GAME DAY

BE A GREAT COMMUNICATOR

DISPLAY RESOLVE & ENTHUSIASM

BE INTOLERANT

1. **Lead by Example.** Be the hardest worker on your team. Put the team's goals ahead of your own in the (very few) instances that the two conflict.

2. **Bring *it* on Game Day.** There are times when you must step up as a leader — game day, late in games, playoffs, etc. You must condition your mind and body to be ready to perform in these moments. You must anticipate and prepare for these moments, and then deliver.

3. **Be a Great Communicator.** Great leaders are great teachers. They understand the power of leverage, so they actively help others. They consistently communicate the team goals and vision. They bridge the gap between players and coaches, and they build relationships between different players. They create synergy.

4. **Display Resolve and Enthusiasm.** Great leaders always believe there is a way to get it done. They never quit on their teammates or their goals. They can take body blows and keep on driving forward. They are not grim, though; they're fun and energetic most of the time. They enjoy life and love the game.

5. **Be *intolerant*.** Great leaders tire of negative people, excuses, and laziness. Great leaders have the courage to say hard, honest things when necessary. Great leaders use *intolerance* as a last resort, but they

understand that it is their responsibility to take a stand when necessary.

Most of all, great leaders know that they are born powerful, no better and no worse than anyone else. They know the mantle of leadership is a choice, not a title, and they own it by earning it, in the service of their teammates and the greater good, one day at a time.

COACHES: Choosing your team captains can be one of the most powerful messages you send your team at any level of competition. The following questions should be asked of your returning players, and then the final team captain decisions should be made by you and your staff.

COACH'S RESOURCE FOR SELECTION OF TEAM CAPTAINS

"It's not the absence of leadership potential that inhibits the development of leaders; it's the persistence of the myth that leadership can't be learned."
~ Jim Kouzes and Barry Posner

Peer Questions Regarding
Demonstrated Leadership Ability
Directions
Answer each of the following questions, listing several current players in no particular order for each.
The names that appear most often reflect the players with the best leadership capabilities:

1. Name the hardest workers on your team.

2. Name the players you trust to make critical plays on offense or defense when the team needs it the most.

3. Who are the best teachers, or most helpful players, on your team?

4. What players make it fun to work hard?

5. If a difficult but honest critical conversation was necessary with an underperforming teammate, what players would be most likely to accomplish that while keeping the situation as positive as possible?

6. What players do you respect the most?

Please contact Bruce at bruce@littleathletesbigleaders.ca for information regarding keynote speeches, parent or community coaching workshops, or other sport specific resources designed to enhance experiential leadership training through organized team sport.

Please visit *www.littleathletesbigleaders.ca* today to sign up for our daily sport excellence message. Many parents share these inspiring, informative messages with their little athletes daily. These wonderful sport parents want to maximize their influence during the youth sport years as they work to raise confident, happy leaders who will do great things in the world.

Appendix 2

CHAPTER NOTES

Introduction

Thompson, Jim, 2009. *Positive Sports Parenting*. Portola Valley, CA: Balance Sports Publishing, LLC., page 5.

Tracy, Brian and Betty B Young, PhD, *How to Raise Happy Healthy Self-Confident Children*, Niles, Illinois: Nightingale Conant audio series.

Dyer, Wayne, PhD, 1996. *What Do You Really Want For Your Children*. Niles, Illinois: Nightingale Conant audio series.

Thompson, Jim, 2009. *Positive Sports Parenting*. Portola Valley, CA: Balance Sports Publishing, LLC., page 7.

Tracy, Brian, *Consider the Consequences*. January 28, 2008 blog: *www.briantracy.com*

Chapter 1

Campbell, D., Ross, MD, 1999. *How to Really Love Your Child*, paper presented at "How to Love a Child — New Insights in Contemporary Psychology. Warsaw, Poland.

Gottman, John, PhD, 2006. *The Four Horsemen of the Apocalypse. http://www.youtube.com/watch?v= CbJPaQY_1dc&feature=player_detailpage*

Gottman, John, PhD, Mar 13, 2007. BetterLifeCoaches *http://wn.com/John_Gottman_The_Magic_ Relationship_Ratio*

Coyle, Daniel, 2009. *The Talent Code*. New York: Bantam Dell, a division of Random House, pages 172–176.

Gallimore, Ron and Tharpe, Roland, 1975–2004. "What a Coach can Teach a Teacher, 1975–2004: Reflections and Reanalysis of John Wooden's Teaching Practices", *Sport Psychologist* 18, no. 2 (2004), 119–37.

Gray, John, PhD., 1999. *Children are From Heaven.* New York: Harper Collins, page 17.

Chapter 2

Eyre, Richard and Linda, Interview with Darren Hardy, Nov 2010. *Family Values*. Lake Dallas, Texas: Success magazine, audio cd.

Positive Coaching Alliance website 2011. *www.positive coach.org*

Dweck, Carol, 2010. *A Growth Mindset About our Talents and Abilities*. Talent Development Resources: *http:// www.youtube.com/watch?v=XHW9l_ sCEyU&feature=player_detailpage#t=152s*

Also Dweck, Carol, 2006. Mindset: The New Psychology of Success. New York, Ballantine Books, a division of Random House, Inc., p72.

Gray, John, PhD., 1999. *Children are From Heaven.* New York: Harper Collins, page 70.

Chapter 4

Ericsson, K Anders, "The Acquisition of Expert Performance: An Introduction to Some of the Issues," in K. Anders Ericsson, ed.,1996. *The Road to Excellence: The Acquisition of Expert Performance in the Arts and Sciences, Sports and Games.* Mahwah, New Jersey: Lawrence Erlbaum Associates.

Pelletier, Luc, PhD, 2010. *Quality of Sport Engagement in Young Athletes: Does the Way You Coach Your Athletes Matter?* Ottawa: 2010 Petro Canada Sport Leadership Conference. *http://23361.vws.magma. ca/sportleadershipsportif/2010/e/presentations/ documents/A2_Pelletier.pdf*

Chapter 6

Gray, John, PhD., 1999. *Children are From Heaven.* New York: Harper Collins, page 7.

Miller, Saul, PhD, 2010. *Performing Under Pressure. http:// www.youtube.com/watch?v=nwddCn3Ngms& feature=player_detailpage#t=36s*

Also Miller, Saul, PhD., 2010. *Performing Under Pressure: Gaining the Mental Edge in Business and Sport.* Mississauga, Ontario: John Wiley and Sons Canada, Ltd.

Miller, Ryan, 2006. *Off the Bench and Into the Game.* Surrey, BC: Heritage Publishing Company, page 40.

Chapter 7

Yaeger, Don, Nov 2010. *Family Values.* Lake Dallas, Texas: Success magazine, page 42.

Chapter 9

Armstrong, Lance and Jenkins, Sally, 2003. *Every Second Counts.* New York: Random House, page 34.

Additional Reading and Resources

There have been some terrific books written in the last few years on achieving excellence in sport, the arts and business. Some of my favorites are:

Bounce: Mozart, Federer, Picasso, Beckham, and the Science of Success by Malcolm Syed, 2010.

The Talent Code: Greatness Isn't Born. It's Grown. Here's How by Daniel Coyle, 2009.

Talent is Overrated: What Really Separates World Class Performers from Everybody Else by Geoff Colvin, 2008, 2010.

Mindset: The New Psychology of Success: Learn How we can Fulfill our Potential by Carol Dweck, 2006.

Outliers: The Story of Success by Malcolm Gladwell, 2008.

My favorite practical little sports book on excellence is *I Can't Accept not Trying* by Michael Jordan and Mark Vancil, 1994.

My favorite autobiography is *Gretzky* by Wayne Gretzky and Rick Reilly, 1990. Sometimes the way we treat greatness, particularly in the early years, is appalling. In this book Wayne's adolescent experiences in Brantford, Ontario can teach all parents how painful jealousy can be for young athletes and their parents.

My favorite "self-help" authors, mostly because of their no-nonsense, practical strategies for personal and business growth, as well as their extensive audio offerings, are Brian Tracy and Jim Rohn.

About the Author

Bruce Beaton played his first ever football game at the age of twenty, and he went on to an outstanding career at Acadia University (BA (hon) MA) and in the CFL and XFL. Bruce went from being a guy in university who had never played football before to eventually being voted to the Edmonton Eskimos All Century team. He became a seven time divisional all-star and a three time league all star player in the CFL.

Bruce began as a struggling player and then became an all-star player and a team leader at every level of football. He played on teams that did not win a game for months then went to win three league championships late in his career.

Bruce has experienced every aspect of team dynamics, and has been exposed to the teachings of over 40 coaches throughout his football career.

Bruce is truly an expert on the subject of habit change, personal standards, and behavior modification. Bruce co-wrote *"The Truth About Success"*, *"Enduring Principles of Leadership"*, and *"Professional Coaching—38 Lessons Learned Through Football"*.

Bruce lives in Kentville, Nova Scotia with his lovely wife Michele and their two beautiful children, Layla and Sam.

CPSIA information can be obtained at www.ICGtesting.com
Printed in the USA
LVOW062028210911

247296LV00001B/12/P